Penllerᵨ

Echoes from Valley

Dedicated to the memory of
Elizabeth 'Betty' Jenkins
1925–2005

First Published 2006

Published by
The Penllergare Trust
Coed Glantawe
Esgairdawe
Llandeilo SA19 7RT

ISBN 0 9536702 3 6

Printed in Wales by
Gwasg Dinefwr Press
Llandybie, Carmarthenshire SA18 3YD

Front cover: Len Beard
Frontispiece: Jennie Eyers
Back cover: Michael Norman

Penllergare

Echoes from Valley Woods

An Anthology

Compiled by

Jennie Eyers

Ymddiriedolaeth Penllergare • The Penllergare Trust

Acknowledgements

Text

The Penllergare Trust wishes to thank all the contributors. We are particularly grateful to Betty Richards for her unpublished memoir *Recollections of an Idyllic Childhood* and to E. Vyron Williams for allowing us to quote from his unpublished *Family Book*.

We would also like to thank Malcolm Hill C.Eng. FICE for permission to quote from his unpublished paper *Penllergaer and the Llewelyns* and, at his request, to acknowledge the debt he owes to the late A. J. Maddox, whose articles in the *South Wales Evening Post* form much of what is known about the Penllergare/Penllergaer locality today.

A. J. Maddox's son, Don Maddox, writes evocatively of his childhood in Penllergaer and the Trust thanks him for his recollections and for generously sharing some of his father's material.

We thank Jennie Bowen too, for allowing us to use extracts from her Penllergaer Primary School project written in 1977 and to quote from her taped interviews.

Images

The source of each picture is indicated next to the image and the Penllergare Trust thanks the following people for the contemporary photographs used in this book: Len Beard, Derek Berry, Jennie Bowen, Keith Clements, Jennifer Cloke, Chris Cray, Eric Hughes, Richard Morris, Jeffrey Phillips, David Whitelock and Arno Wolff.

We also thank the many people who have kindly allowed us to copy photographs from their family albums and to publish paintings, drawings and photographs of Penllergare in their ownership. We refer to these works as from 'private collections'. We are grateful to the Royal Commission on the Ancient and Historical Monuments of Wales for permission to use the realisation of the Walled Gardens. The Trust also appreciates the photographic assistance of Jonathan Bayes in reproducing JDL's Chapel of Ease painting.

Penllergare, Echoes from Valley Woods is a compilation of personal recollections. The Penllergare Trust therefore cannot vouch for the accuracy of material within individual contributions.

Llywodraeth Cynulliad Cymru
Welsh Assembly Government

All profits from the sale of this book go towards the work of the Penllergare Trust and its Community and Education programme.

Contents

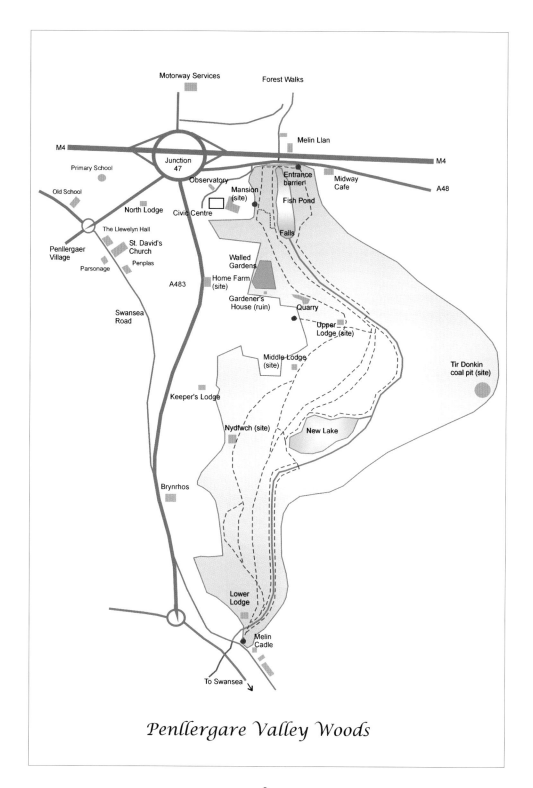

Penllergare Valley Woods

Autumn mist over the River Llan

Introduction

Penllergare is a former gentry estate on the north-west fringe of Swansea. Now in dereliction it has a uniquely important place in the culture and history of South Wales.

This anthology is not a definitive history of Penllergare but a collection of impressions spanning nearly 200 years. It includes recollections of people who lived, worked, courted and played in this valley, the kaleidoscope of characters whose lives were touched by the place and many of whose descendants walk here today. The voices of the past interweave with those of the present, sharing the common bond that is a deep affection for Penllergare Valley Woods.

We have deliberately avoided a strict chronological order, preferring to explore Penllergare more thematically, mixing the decades, the months and the centuries. It is good to know we can stand alongside John Dillwyn Llewelyn, Ikey the gamekeeper, Thereza, Charles Richards the butler, young Reg Blackwell, Emma Thomasina or Mr. Nunns the head-gardener; if not in life then certainly on the page, seeing through their eyes.

The memories and reminiscences have been gathered from letters, diaries and accounts of visits, some written privately others for publication. The Penllergare Trust has also invited people to write their recollections and has collected many oral accounts of 'life in the old days' in recorded conversations. For people who were unable to obtain a copy of our first publication, *Penllergare, A Victorian Paradise* by Richard Morris, we have included here short biographies of the three men – father, son and grandson – who were responsible for the burgeoning of Penllergare, and to help put the rest into context. The younger people in the locality have made their contribution too and we have included their observations, poems and paintings, in what we hope is a celebration of Penllergare Valley Woods in all its moods, in all its seasons.

Jennie Eyers

Rhododendrons and Monkey Puzzle

The Trust would particularly like to thank the following people. Vanda Morton for allowing us to quote from the journals of Thereza Story Maskelyne (née Dillwyn Llewelyn) and to Dr. David Painting for permission to quote from Amy Dillwyn's diaries that are currently in his ownership. Richard Morris, as ever, has been generous in allowing us access to his research, his photographic collection and to his Dillwyn Llewelyn archive. My personal thanks goes to Hilary M. Thomas, our consultant editor, for her invaluable guidance and wise advice.

This is not the place for a discussion on nomenclature and the Trust is well aware of the differing views held both locally and further afield of the spelling of the estate's name. For this reason we include an extract from Jeff Childs's paper on that subject *'Penllergare or Penllergaer'* (first published in *Morgannwg. The Journal of Glamorgan History, Vol. XLVII 2003*) in the Appendix and we are grateful to him for allowing us to quote both this and from other work. For the sake of consistency and to avoid confusion, the name of the mansion, gardens and parkland belonging to the Dillwyn Llewelyn family are referred to as Penllergare and the village and the surrounding area, as Penllergaer.

The Trust would like to emphasise that this book could not have been produced without our contributors, or be so wonderfully illustrated. It has been a community project and people have been generous in their support. We requested permission to quote (and publish illustrations) from all our sources but if anyone has inadvertently been omitted, we apologise unreservedly.

For their much-appreciated contributions to the costs of publication we are indebted to David Andrews, Dr. Stuart Jenkins and Jennifer Woods; to the Lottery-funded programme 'Awards for All Wales', the Cadw Civic Initiatives (Heritage) Grant Scheme, the Ethel and Gwynne Morgan Charitable Trust (long-time supporters of the Penllergare project), the Better Swansea Compact Development Fund; and to West Glamorgan Archive Service for an interest-free loan.

Finally, our very special thanks goes to our Chairman, Hal Moggridge, for not only agreeing to write the Foreword but also for finding time in his exceedingly busy life to do it so aptly and so elegantly. Hal is one of the foremost landscape architects of our time with a body of work that includes the Royal Parks in London, RHS Gardens Wisley, Blenheim Park, Aberglasney, Dinefwr Park and the National Botanic Garden of Wales. The Trust is indeed fortunate to have at its helm a man of such remarkable expertise.

Jennie Eyers
The Penllergare Trust, 2006

Foreword

My great uncle Traherne, a frequent childhood visitor to Penllergare in the 1850s, wrote to his brother in 1870 describing a train journey along the recently opened railway through the Alps from Innsbruck to Italy:

> '*The many tunnels interposed intervals between these varied scenes, which were not unlike those rather nervous periods of darkness when the slides of the Penllergare magic-lantern were being changed, and when, the light being turned off, a pale flickering reflection came from the white sheet, which would stir in unnatural ways, as if it concealed phantoms behind it – and, like these intervals also, were succeeded by exquisite pictures.*'

This delightful book similarly evokes with words a series of remembered scenes of Penllergare, widely varied personal memories which bring the place to life. Readers will discover the grounds being created in the 1840s, birds, flowers and reptiles living in the woods and gardens in the twentieth century, charming poems and remarks by primary school children of today and much, much else. This collection of impressions oozes affection for and delight in Penllergare even in its present dilapidated condition.

In recent years invasive vegetation has concealed much within Penllergare Valley Woods and the derelict garden structures around the former house; they have become like the imagined phantoms behind the white sheet upon which John Dillwyn Llewelyn projected slides of his photographs. But the phantoms of Valley Woods are real. When the overgrowth is cleared features from the old photographs reappear, ready to be repaired and replanted. Therefore the Echoes in these pages are more than reflections about the past. They are also a call demanding that Penllergare is restored to captivate future generations with all its charms, its nineteenth century moods, its twenty-first century values as a landscape for future generations from Swansea, Gower and all South Wales.

Hal Moggridge
OBE, VMH, PPLI, FIHort, RIBA, AAdipl.
Chairman of the Penllergare Trust

Jennifer Cloke

Upper Lake in winter, looking north

First Encounters

This place . . . It's awesome!
Unknown teenage boy at the waterfall, October 2005.

We closed our eyes and listened and all we heard was nature. Birds, small rustling noises; it was beautiful.
Vicky Brown, Penllergaer Primary School, 2003.

Years of wonder and delight are the memories of my childhood at Penllergare. It was a magical place.
Betty Richards, March 2006.

As a youngster I always had an amazing sense of happiness whenever I was at Penllergare.
D. I. Hughes, October 2005.

Penllergare was my playground of delight, discovery and learning for ten years.
Yvonne Colman, March 2006.

For beauty and scenery there is nothing in the whole land of Morgannwg to excel Penllergare.
The South Wales Daily News, 20th August 1910.

. . . to those who visit Penllergare its great attraction will be its horticulture and . . . what is I believe its chief glory, its rhododendrons.
H. Honeywood D'Dombrain, *The Gardener's Magazine*, 21st September 1895.

The Drive

Richard Morris

The Finest Site of Natural Beauty

Upper Lake. Mid 1850s
Photograph by John Dillwyn Llewelyn

The residence of J. T. D. Llewelyn Esq. stands on one of the finest sites for natural beauty that could be found in the county of Glamorgan. The elevation is some 300 feet above the level of the sea. The house, a commodious building of two storeys, commands extensive views from all sides, embracing rock, wood, water, hill and dale and rich pasture land. The principal entrance to the demesne is a mile and a half from the Cockett station on the Great Western Railway and about four miles from the town of Swansea. The private approach is a mile and a half in length. It is conducted through the park and along the breast of a wooded hill, and cut out of the solid rock in many places. As it ascends the hill the scenery increases in grandeur till the house is reached. On the left the ground rises a considerable height above the drive, and on the right it descends far down to the valley, where flows the river Llan, a rapid trout stream, which passes through two lakes at different levels as it winds its way through the picturesque grounds of Penllergare on its course to the sea. The banks on both sides of the valley are covered in heavy timber principally oaks in the best of health, while here and there large trees of Hemlock Spruce (*Abies canadensis*), *Taxodium sempervirens*, *Wellingtonia gigantea* and *Cryptomeria japonica* stand out in bold relief, lit up in many places by a glorious undergrowth of the best species and varieties of rhododendrons and hardy azaleas, some of which are of large dimensions and in the most luxuriant health, the soil and situation being favourable to their growth.

Andrew Pettigrew
The Journal of Horticulture and Cottage Gardener
June/July 1886

The Beautiful Valley

You are now approaching the beautiful valley in which Penllergare is situated, and as you pass within its gates, Swansea and all its surroundings and smoke are shut from your view. The avenue leading up to the house is no prim, formal arrangement of rows of trees but a beautiful half-wild combination of all kinds of lovely things.

As you approach the house, which is situated on elevated ground, you see below you on the right hand the river with its waterfall and the lakes which it has been made to form, while the sides of the valley are clothed with trees. There are two seasons when Penllergare must be especially lovely; in the early spring when the trees are bursting into their fresh green foliage, and the rhododendrons are all ablaze with their gorgeous

Rhododendrons

Jennie Eyers

and beautiful flowers; and in the autumn when the tints of the fading foliage lend such a charm to our woodland scenery.

H. Honeywood D'Dombrain
The Gardener's Magazine
21st September 1895

My First Visit

Penllergare Valley Woods is a beautiful place and we visited it for the first time in September. There are lots of different kinds of plants and trees like the Monkey Puzzle. There is also a man-made waterfall and a bridge going over a quarry. There is a lot of wildlife like rabbits, fish in the river and lots of birds. We walked down a long drive that John Dillwyn Llewelyn made for his visitors. There is also an Observatory where John Dillwyn Llewelyn took one of the first photographs of the moon.

Bethan Bedford
Year 6, Pontlliw Primary School
2005

In the Beginning

Around thirty years ago I made my first visit to Penllergare. I was very interested to see the actual estate having known some of the photographs by John Dillwyn Llewelyn, through an album that once belonged to Bessie Dillwyn and had been passed down to my mother-in-law by Amy Dillwyn. At that time there had been a generation gap, and though my mother-in-law told me she had been to Penllergare in the distant past, she did not know the present generation of the Dillwyn Llewelyn family. On that first visit with my wife Sue, we were able to drive up from Cadle along the driveway as far as the remains of one of the lodges. We then walked on further to the remains of the house and picked up a piece of stone from the ruins.

Some years pass and I take an interest in the photography of John Dillwyn Llewelyn. Luckily I was encouraged by Margaret Harker, a colleague where I worked, who knew a past President of the Royal Photographic Society. Through Margaret I was allowed access to the RPS library, and it was there that I first discovered the importance of JDL as a photographic pioneer.

One day I received information about an article in the first Journal of the (Royal) Horticultural Society describing an orchid house that JDL had built at Penllergare, and following a visit to the Linnean Society (of which John had been a Fellow) I soon acquired a copy. But nobody I contacted was able to tell me where this building lay until one day I received via David Painting, then in the Library of Swansea University, a letter from a Mr. Eady who was living in the restored Lower Lodge. In wandering round the estate, he had come across a well-hidden area surrounded by an immense wall within which was a strange structure. He sent me a videotape of their perambulations. He had discovered the remains of the Orchid House and on one of those typical Welsh days, sudden mixtures of rain and sun, I went to meet the Eadys. We set off across the fields up to the Walled Garden area taking with us a photocopy of the diagram from the RHS Journal. The Orchid House was difficult to recognise at first and there was one puzzle. Though the plan matched what I saw, where there should have been a pond in the middle there was in fact a raised bed with a brick surround. I was told later that John's son, JTDL, was a great grower of camellias and if I had asked locally for the camellia house it might have jerked memories.

It was then suggested that I should contact Michael Powell of Rees Richards, the family estate agents, and find out what they might know. Michael wrote me one of his, apparently famous, letters, 'I hear what you say but . . . the Orchid House was attached to the main mansion.' This was not where I had identified it. Michael agreed to meet me at the site and duly arrived in his pink shirt and armed with a saw. He had to agree with me that this was the site of the building and we duly set to work to try and clear some of the vegetation. We also investigated the brick wall around the central cistern and found that the bricks were quite loose and, when taken down, there was the solid stone surround to the original pond.

Move on again to about twelve years ago when the BJ Group were in possession of a lease to build on parts of the estate and, in return, were to create a country park on the

Private collection

The Drive. Photograph by John Dillwyn Llewelyn. Mid 1850s

rest of it. My concern was that they apparently had permission to build within the Walled Garden area, the site of the Orchid House! I desperately needed to find out just how important an area this was, so letters flew in all directions: the National Trust, Kew Gardens, the Royal Horticultural Society and Cadw. It was not long before I was being told that, if indeed this was the site of the Orchid House, it was of the greatest historical importance. One of my letters was to The Welsh Historic Gardens Trust and landed on, or near, the desk of Michael Norman. The rest, as they say, is now history . . .

Richard Morris
2005

The Forgotten Heritage

In the early 1990s Wales was waking up to the fact that it too had its share of historic parks and gardens. So when Richard Morris's letter arrived on my desk at The Welsh Historic Gardens Trust I realised that Penllergare was almost certainly part of that forgotten heritage.

Andrew Sclater (historic landscape consultant) was asked to make a quick recce and my first memories are of a bitterly cold day in January 1991, scrambling with him along remnants of paths and terraces engulfed in laurel and rhododendron. His report noted that the landscape design was, '. . . essentially simple, yet highly sophisticated . . . which contrasted magnificence and intimacy, drama and serenity'. Confirmation came in Cadw's Register where Penllergare is described as, 'The partial survival of a very important picturesque and romantic landscape of the mid-nineteenth century, the creation of John Dillwyn Llewelyn . . .'

Chris Cray

River Llan and bamboo

Copper beeches in spring

However, already derelict and top-sliced by the M4 motorway the site now faced new threats. In return for housing development on the margins the developers were to lay out a country park in the valley itself but it was soon evident that they wouldn't be able to meet their obligations. Although we managed to persuade the Council to withdraw permission for building in the Walled Gardens we were faced with the all-too familiar dilemma: no question that Penllergare should be saved, but who was to do it, and where was the money to come from?

And there it rested more or less until 1999 when we founded the Friends of Penllergare and published Richard Morris's book, *Penllergare, A Victorian Paradise*, to raise public consciousness of the importance of the place. Encouraged by its run-away success and galvanised by the destruction of part of the Walled Garden complex by the house-builders, we formed the Penllergare Trust as an independent charity in May 2000 to champion the protection, conservation and restoration of this cultural landscape. There was an argument with the Charity Commission over the use of the word 'cultural'. They preferred 'historical' but we persevered because we felt that the people associated with Penllergare were as important as the place itself.

Richard Morris and David Harris were founder Trustees, together with Hal Moggridge, the eminent historic landscape consultant, with his familial connections with Penllergare. Philip James of the National Trust joined them in 2004.

Michael Norman
2006

Cool

I really enjoyed visiting the woods, it was exciting. I never knew so many different types of birds used the woods and that there were sixty-three types last year. The man-made waterfall was cool. The Monkey Puzzle tree was funny and the forest would look better if you got rid of that plant [*Himalayan Balsam*] that is on its way to Tesco.

Sam Lockley
Llangyfelach Primary School
2005

On My Way to Penllergaer

There was a time when the name 'Penllergaer' would fill me with panic. In the early 1950s I was living in Sketty and attending junior school in the Uplands and I would travel between these two points on the bus. The United Welsh buses went from Swansea to Killay and south Gower and also to north Gower via Penllergaer and these two routes diverged in the Uplands. Occasionally I would see the bus waiting outside Wayne's store in the Uplands and jump on board without looking at the destination on its front, and then hold my breath until it passed the junction of Sketty Road and Glanmor Road. If it took the right-hand route up the hill – panic stations! I was on my way to Penllergaer, which, to eight-year-old me, could have been on the moon!

Many years passed and in 2000 I found myself living in the place whose name I had once dreaded. I had heard vague stories about a valley walk hidden somewhere near the M4 junction 47, but it wasn't until the vendor of our house, which is built on the site of the Home Farm, introduced me to the Penllergare Estate that I became interested in finding out more about its location and history.

Firstly I bought the book *Penllergare, A Victorian Paradise* by Richard Morris. My husband and I then started walking in the valley on Sunday mornings and trying to pinpoint the exact locations of the photographs in the book. We were struck by its apparent remoteness, despite its closeness to the motorway. I remember worrying a bit about the kind of people we were likely to run into in this secluded place and deciding it was certainly not somewhere I would choose to walk alone.

We had visited Aberglasney in its early stages of restoration and it crossed our minds that the same could be done for Penllergare. Then we heard about the guided walks organised by The Penllergare Trust. In the years since we have endeavoured to keep abreast of its tireless efforts to find a way to restore Valley Woods to some semblance of its former glory as one of Swansea's most important estates, and make it even more accessible and interesting as a country park. For our part, we do our best to introduce as many people as possible to the valley and its history – and all our visitors have their photograph taken by the Waterfall!

Jennifer Cloke
2005

Private collection

Four Oaks. 1853
Photograph by John Dillwyn Llewelyn

Looking towards the Waterfall

Discovery

In about 1982 when my children were old enough to cope with walking outdoors without difficulty, we decided that the part of the Penllergare estate behind the motorway services would be an ideal place in which to go in search of adventure.

It was returning from one of these forays that we saw an entry point off the A48 near the Midway Café. As we entered we discovered a scene of devastation with carved blocks of sandstone littering a large area that appeared to be the remains of an imposing building. Our first attempt to explore was to try and reach the origin of the sound of water that could be heard below us in the valley. It was a miserable failure because, after forcing our way into a very dense mixture of bramble, rhododendron and nettles, we were halted by a drop in land surface that we now know to be the terrace walls, but was then an impassable thicket. This was over twenty years after the mansion was destroyed.

During the following months we visited the site more frequently and were able to find old paths, animal tracks and make our own paths through the still dense overgrowth. We found by accident walls, sets of steps and the remains of buildings long ravaged by time but very interesting for children to understand that people had been living and working in the area for at least two hundred years.

Keith Clements
April 2005

I Find My Valley

My parents were bombed out of their house during the war and ended up for a time living at Ashley Road Army Camp at Derwen Fawr. My first visit to Penllergare was when I was about eighteen months old with the Bible College of Wales. I think they felt

18

sorry for us kids because they often gave us treats. Haile Selassie, the Emperor of Ethiopia, was staying there at the time. He was a great friend of the principal Rees Howells. Haile Selassie was my godfather. The men-folk were either away working or still in the Services and there was no one else and he took rather a shine to me. I think it was because I was the only little boy; all the other children were girls. My mother told me she has a vivid memory of me one Christmas sitting on the Emperor's knees singing 'Away in a Mangle'. Uncle Toby was my other godfather and it was he who brought us up for day trips to Penllergare.

Terrace steps to the Upper Lake

We came in off the Swansea Road through Home Farm which we called Ten Town because it had ten buildings around the yard. Then we went on to Graig Nydfwch Wood, which we had named Fern Hill, why I do not know. In the early 1950s farms on the south-east of the Penllergare estate were being released for development because there was such a shortage of housing. It was on one of these trips that Uncle Toby said to my Dad, "That's where you want to live" and he pointed across the valley. They were just beginning to build the houses at Blaen-y-Maes. It used to be a tenant farm of the estate. At that time the farm buildings were still standing, the house and barns arranged around a large yard and a Monkey Puzzle tree in front of the house. The people hadn't long gone because there were still chickens running about the place.

My family came to live at Blaen-y-Maes when I was four years old and I think I discovered Penllergare Valley Woods the very next day. At that time my father was an acrobat in the circus and he needed somewhere to practise. There was no room at home and seeing these nearby woods, we all trooped over with him. There were only four of us then, three sisters and myself, but eventually I was one of nine children. The first time we went exploring Dad led the way. He was in front and my Mum behind carrying one, if not two, of my sisters. We scrambled down the east bank and could hear the Waterfall but couldn't find it because it was all so overgrown, nor did we find the steps. He continued straight up the opposite hillside through the boggy ground that must have been the top lake until we discovered the mansion. It was in a bad state, the slates were off the roof, you could see the rafters and it was open to the sky.

The first spring we were here we could not believe our eyes when we looked over the valley to Penllergare. The top of the hillside was a vivid blue. There were acres and acres of bluebells and lower down rhododendrons of every colour imaginable. It was a mass of colour and it drew you towards it. You couldn't resist the place.

David Whitelock
in conversation, 2006

19

A Walk and a Picnic

Penllergare is celebrated for its rhododendrons, and here the family may be studied from the small European species to the massive and wide-stretching clumps of the exogens which have now become as familiar to our own as native productions . . . Among the azaleas, Mr. Llewelyn [*John Talbot Dillwyn Llewelyn*] points out a newly introduced species from Japan, which is quite hardy enough to flourish out of doors in our climate, and which, though the range of its blooms is not yet fully developed in point of view, promises to become a great favourite . . . The walk was then extended to the banks of the Upper Lake, and the Waterfall. The waters of the Llan stream, in their passage through the Penllergare cwm or valley, have been dammed up in two places, forming a couple of

Jennie Eyers

Monkey Puzzle

sinuous lakes, the larger of which is no less than thirty acres in extent, and holds about as much water as one of our great storage reservoirs at Velindre. The burgesses of Swansea, who have had to pay to the tune of £80,000 each for their reservoirs will learn with something like wonder that the cost of constructing the Penllergare Lake did not exceed £2,000.

The waterlilies which now so luxuriate in the smooth waters, were successfully transplanted here in the face of the most discouraging views of the florists. Mr. J. D. Llewelyn, pere, got some of the lilies dug up from the Crymlin Bog, placed with their mud in wicker baskets, and then dropped them, baskets and all, into Penllergare lake, where their rope-like stems, and platter leaves, and chased inflorescents now gladden the eye. From the upper to the lower lake the water falls in a picturesque cascade in a

Chris Cray

Colonising rhododendrons

romantic rockery which is half hidden in the trees. In the walk by the waterside the most superficial observer cannot fail to notice the great variety of the trees; oak and ash and elm, sycamore and beech and birch, poplar and willow and pine, firs and 'monkeys' . . . A fine chalybeate spring bubbles up under the trees, whereat some of the picnickers stooped to drink . . .

It would take long to tell of the Hospital and Convalescent Home which Mr. Llewelyn maintains in his grounds, but which he did not show his visitors. Here the poor people of the whole countryside get medical advice and relief gratis, and in cases of fever or accident some five or six in-patients can be housed. Many of the picnickers thoroughly enjoyed a peep down into the fox kennel, a large walled-in quarry, where the family of Reynard are bred and fed, and kept ready for the chase . . .

A few walked off quietly through the beautiful avenue of sycamores and elms to the silent church and the slumberous churchyard. Here encircled by cultured foliage, lie the remains of some of the Llewelyn family.

Picnic at Penllergare
by Working Men's Club
The Cambrian, 1st July 1881

Such a Lovely Place

I didn't have a clue who John Dillwyn Llewelyn was until the walk. I was sorry to hear about the vandalism because it is such a lovely place. The plants were very interesting especially the Monkey Puzzle tree. I enjoyed counting the steps and it was strange that so many people counted different numbers. When I come back I would like to see an assault course amongst the trees involving a lot of mud!

Thomas Frayne
Llangyfelach Primary School
2005

Jennifer Cloke

Copper beech in spring

Lewis Weston Dillwyn
(1778–1855)

The Dillwyn family appears to have originated, or at least to have taken their name from the village of Dilwyn on the road between Weobley and Leominster in Herefordshire, but in the seventeenth century they settled at Llangorse in Breconshire.

Lewis Weston Dillwyn was the great grandson of William Dillwyn who had become a Quaker and had emigrated with his friend William Penn in 1699 where, being a surveyor, he was employed on the planning and building of Philadelphia. His father, also William Dillwyn, had returned to England in 1774 where, in 1777, he married Sarah, the daughter and heiress of Lewis Weston of High Hall, Essex. Lewis Weston Dillwyn was born at Hackney, London, on 21st August 1778.

It is recorded that in February of 1788 Dillwyn was left at Foster's School where he commenced as a boarder aged nine. Dillwyn's health at that time was indifferent and he was sent to Folkestone in an attempt to improve it. When he was twenty years old he went to Dover and began his great study of plant life, a list of which was read to the Linnean Society in March 1801. In 1802 he started to write his first botanical work, *The Natural History of British Confervae*, which he completed in 1809. Also in 1802, when he was living at Walthamstow, his father purchased for him a controlling interest in the Cambrian Pottery on the Strand in Swansea and placed him in charge. In June 1802 he settled in the town permanently and lived at Burrows Lodge.

In 1804, at the early age of twenty-six he was elected a Fellow of the Royal Society. Dillwyn's first zoological work was *The Descriptive Catalogue of Recent Shells* which was printed in two volumes. It was published in 1817 and was well received by the various scientific bodies.

The most notable incident in Dillwyn's private life was his marriage in 1807 to Mary, the only child of John Llewelyn of Penllergare. The Llewelyn family, originally of Ynysygerwn, near Neath, had acquired the Penllergare estate on the extinction of the Price family in about 1790. In 1817 Dillwyn relinquished his active interest in the Cambrian Pottery by leasing it for a term of years. By this time it was a great success and Swansea China had gained worldwide renown.

In 1818 he became High Sheriff for Glamorgan, having previously been a magistrate for a number of years. In 1832, after previous refusals to stand, he was elected a Member of Parliament of the first Reform Parliament. He is prominent in the painting of the First Reform Parliament of 1832 by Hayter, which hangs in the National Portrait Gallery. Dillwyn is seated to the left of the Speaker and with him is Christopher Rice Mansel Talbot, first cousin to Henry Fox Talbot and the brother of Emma, who was to marry Dillwyn's son John. His parliamentary career was not a long one and he retired in 1837 on the accession of Queen Victoria. The freedom of the Borough of Swansea was conferred upon him in 1834, and from 1835 to 1840 he served as Alderman and ultimately as Mayor of Swansea. At the same time he took a close interest in all matters in the locality as well as fulfilling his duties as squire at Penllergare.

Among other benevolent actions, Lewis Weston Dillwyn established a free day school in the grounds of his estate for the rudimentary education of children from the village and surrounding area. The school, built by Dillwyn and maintained at the family's expense, was a stone, one floor structure comprised of one large room. In the early days, members of the Dillwyn family assisted with the teaching.

Apart from his connection with the famous Swansea porcelain Lewis Weston Dillwyn became a prominent figure, both locally and nationally, as a man of learning and an enthusiastic and zestful supporter of all cultural, scientific and educative movements. He was the author of several important works on natural history and in 1838 was one of the founders of the Royal Institution of South Wales.

Lewis Weston Dillwyn kept his personal diary for over thirty-five years and the contents reveal how wide his scientific and cultural interests were, that he was a humane, compassionate, generous man and a humble, devout Christian. He appears to have ceased to belong to the Society of Friends on his marriage and he worshipped thereafter in the Established Church.

As the squire he had a deep and genuine concern for the health and welfare of the ordinary people, living in the area surrounding Penllergare House. Accompanied by Mary, his wife, he would often walk about Cors Eynon to inspect the state of the poor, even visiting nearby farms to see some children suffering from smallpox.

Although it does not appear that Dillwyn ever experienced any financial difficulties, he found living at Penllergare House very expensive and regretted that his expenditure was so great. The expenditure for his first year at the mansion was exactly £2,616-7s-9½d. and exceeded what Dillwyn wished it to be. This had increased from £1,040 for the previous year as had the consumption of beer from 738 to 3,289 gallons!

As vice-president of the British Association for the Advancement of Science, he welcomed the Association to Swansea in 1848. To mark this special occasion Dillwyn produced *The Flora and Fauna of Swansea* which was his last literary work. After this his health declined and in November 1849 he was attacked by a congestion of the brain which resulted in his gradually withdrawing from outdoor pursuits and spending his final years in peaceful retirement. His last visit to Penllergare was in July 1852 when he, 'ventured on a drive in the phaeton across the Cockett to Penllergare'. He died at Sketty Hall on the 31st August 1855 at the age of seventy-seven, leaving his widow Mary, two sons and two daughters.

The Dictionary of National Biography describes him as, 'thoroughly upright in all his dealings, and a liberal and active country gentleman'. He was a distinguished man of distinct ability, who was devoted to his family, his scientific interests and the public duties that his position entailed. More remarkably, his son, John Dillwyn Llewelyn was to exhibit similar characteristics and extend the influence, philanthropy and reputation of the family at Penllergare.

Malcolm Hill, C.Eng. FICE
An extract from *Penllergaer and the Llewelyns*

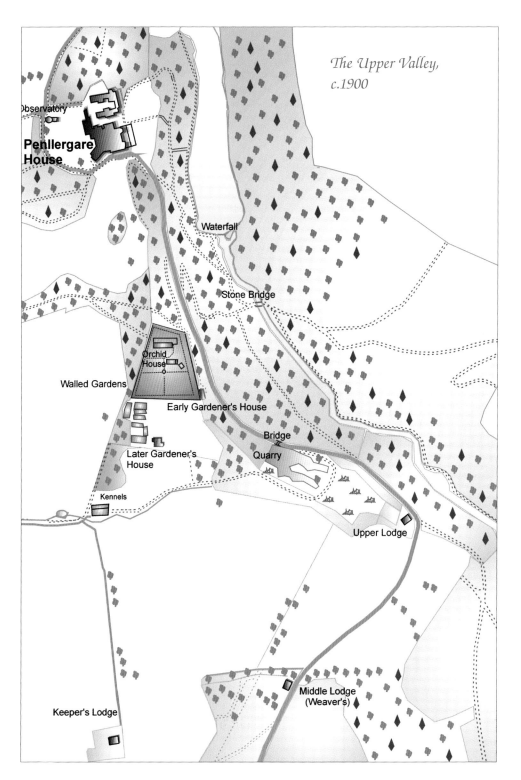

The Upper Valley, c.1900

Observatory

Penllergare House

Waterfall

Stone Bridge

Orchid House

Walled Gardens

Early Gardener's House

Bridge

Later Gardener's House

Quarry

Kennels

Upper Lodge

Keeper's Lodge

Middle Lodge (Weaver's)

Big House and Little Homes

My dear Mamma

[Extract from a letter to her mother Lady Mary Cole.]

I have been so very busy since my return home that I have never written to you – John has some pretty Orchises coming to blow in the stove – one is to have yellow and red flowers with long tails 2 or 3 inches long, and they show already in a curious manner, altho' the spike of blossoms has only just begun to form the buds . . . Our scarlet rhododendron will be finer this year than it was last year when you saw it and the *arboreum*, which is crimson, is covered this year for the first time with flower buds.

Our house is advanced so far that the masons are gone and the plasterers & carpenters are in full employment – one room, the butler's pantry, is available for our use and we have been glad to begin making use of it as a place to put some of the cram of furniture into – the portico is half up & the frost is the only hindrance to its progress but I suppose they won't go on with it till the rain as well as the frost is past – I mean the winter gone – I have a beautiful *Epacris* and two *Justicia Flavicoma*, *Grevillia rosmarinifolia*, *Covicea speciosa* and a white camellia etc. etc. including the beauty which Mary brought us from London last year with eight flower buds on it and in high health.

John has not fallen to at any great job since our return home as the frost has hardly been enough out of the ground. They are busy in the garden setting up the two old hothouses again, which were not done before and laying some nice water pipes from the Farm pond to supply the boilers and to have rocks in the garden. Everybody is ill with the influenza in the neighbourhood and my poor schoolmistress is very unwell – our household is well – Babes are both quite well.

I am your affectionate daughter
Emma

Emma Thomasina Dillwyn Llewelyn
18th January 1837

Private collection

Emma and John Dillwyn Llewelyn, c.1850

A Desirable Residence

Penllergare is situated about five miles from what is called the flourishing – but at the same time smoky – city of Swansea and, as its name implies, is an old Cymrick or Celtic home, for *gare* signified, I believe, the head of the camp of fortified earthworks that the old Celtic inhabitants of Cambria raised, and Tredegar means foot of the camp.

Penllergare House,
c.1900

. . . The house itself is a comparatively modern structure, the older part of it being perhaps two hundred or three hundred years old, while the modern part of the house dates back to the earlier days of this century. It is therefore more remarkable for its comfort than for any claim to architectural beauty; but whatever that may be, I am sure it would not be forgotten in its beautiful environments, wood and water, hill and dale, all conspiring to make a picture of real sylvan beauty.

H. Honeywood D' Dombrain
The Gardener's Magazine
21st September 1895

The Conservatory

The conservatory, a substantially built half-spanroofed structure, is slightly curved in its length to suit the wing of the building to which it is attached. It is about sixty feet long, twenty feet high, and broad in proportion, with a fountain and beds in the centre, and a narrow stage at the side of the path round the back wall. The wall is covered with camellias and orange trees, and the bed in the centre of the house is planted with large camellias, tree ferns and other greenhouse plants. Fuchsias and various climbers cover the rafters in front, and hang down in graceful festoons. The house contained a general collection of greenhouse plants which were clean and healthy, and everything looked neat and orderly. Besides the plants in the conservatory, the entrance hall of the mansion was neatly furnished with a miscellaneous collection of flowering plants amongst which were a batch of well-grown plants of an extra fine strain of *Calceolaria.*

Mr. Llewelyn devotes a great deal of time to the pursuit of natural history. He is a good entomologist, a keen florist, hybridiser and arboriculturist, and it is but right to say he is ably assisted in horticulture and arboriculture by his genial and intelligent gardener, Mr. Warmington.

Andrew Pettigrew
The Journal of Horticulture and Cottage Gardener
June/July 1886

George and Betty Richards at the front door of Penplas

Life begins at Penplas

Our family became associated originally with Penllergare when my father, Robert Charles Richards, joined the staff of Sir John Talbot Dillwyn Llewelyn as his butler in 1907. My father had been brought up in the country and was already very knowledgeable on country matters; he was a good shot and a good fisherman and always acted as Sir John's loader when he went shooting. At that time the Penllergare estate was very well run with a large staff working inside the house and many outside workers. Most of the staff were from the locality and the Llewelyns looked after their tenants well. They paid regular visits to their house in Cromwell Gardens, London and entertained family and friends at Penllergare.

On July 31st 1916, Sir John fell and broke his leg badly and was incapacitated for over twenty-one weeks. It was at this time that an extra passenger lift was installed at Penllergare, in the stair well of the 'brown staircase' which went up from just below the Smoking Room to the passage outside Sir John's bedroom. My father was very close to Sir John over this time, as letters written by Sir John show how much he appreciated all the care and attention given. He recovered quite well from the accident and continued being active.

My parents married in May 1917 and after a short time were offered Penplas to live in. Penplas was a lovely stone built house on the edge of the estate. It was next to St. David's Church and had a large garden. The front drive went around an oval shrubbery with a path leading off through a grassy area on the right where we kept our chickens. The vegetable garden on the left ran behind the house down to the field between the churchyard and us. The gate at the end of the path opened onto the pathway leading to the Tennis Garden and Penllergare House. On the opposite side of Penplas was a thick colourful hedge with the main road leading from Swansea to Carmarthen behind it. On the opposite side of the road were only three houses. One was the Parsonage and a large semi-detached property made of stone. The road went slightly up hill from the village and at the crest, steps had been formed into the steep bank from the road on our side leading up to a stone stile. This was known as 'Sticklemount'. A few trees formed a glade just inside the hedge and a path led across the park to the stone road leading from Penllergare House up to the Iron Gate on the Swansea Road. Where the path met the stone road, it continued as a solid black road to the Home Farm and was formed from compacted coal dust. Just below this, on the park, was the Cricket Field with an excellent pavilion and well-kept pitch on which many well-known cricketers had played.

My brother, George Owen, was born at Penplas in 1921 and I came along in 1923, Hannah Elizabeth, and by all accounts was always very active. Mrs. Mount, Sir John's younger daughter, Gladys, was my godmother.

27

I recall only one occasion when I met a very old gentleman whom I had seen in the Observatory Garden at Penllergare and I was later taken into the Library to see. It was around my birthday for he gave me five shillings (This must, I feel, have been my third birthday). I had no idea who the kind old gentleman was!

Betty Richards
2005

Little Homes

The estate had three lodges. The Vaughan family lived in North Lodge that was next door to the Sunday School. It was the responsibility of that family to keep the fires lit during the winter months for Sunday School where Miss Vaughan was the teacher-in-charge and this lady had an inexplicable hold on my life in ensuing years. The Coles, who were distantly related and friends of the Llewelyn family, occupied the Upper Lodge on the estate's main drive to Cadle Mill. I used to know Betty Cole who was at the same school as Hubert my elder brother. There was also another lodge at the Cadle end entrance but I didn't know the people living here.

The grounds around the Big House were very beautiful and bisected by the River Llan with waterfalls and lakes throughout the length of the estate. One of these lakes had a boathouse and a boat, which I sometimes used to take out onto the lake but it leaked and needed frequent baling out. The lakes had large groups of water lilies with beautiful flowers in different pastel shades. The entrance to the estate off the [*now*] A48 near the road-bridge over the River Llan had large cast iron gates with the family crest. On the opposite side of the road was the continuation of the estate that led down a stone drive to Melin Llan and this entrance too had cast iron gates of similar design with the family crest on. This gate was the entrance to Tyle Du (The Black Hills), the Twyn and Melin Llan. I believe the metal gates at all entrances were requisioned in 1940-41 for the war effort.

Private collection

Penllergare House. Watercolour by Louise Senyk, 2005

In the early 19th century Lewis Weston Dillwyn built a school at the north west corner of the estate that later became the girls' school and then the Sunday School. The cottage, North Lodge, on the left, was originally built for the schoolteacher

There was a stone bridge a distance of about half a mile at the bottom of this drive where the Elsden family lived in a beautiful spot overlooking the River Llan. The house was built on a rock promontory. Joan Elsden and Stan who lived here were friends of mine. Another house on the opposite side of the drive was almost at the river's edge and this was where Mrs. Lloyd lived. Mrs. Lloyd used the river water to wash clothes and obtained drinking water from a well near the house. She lived alone, was a retired teacher and a water colour and oil painter of some distinction. This house was at one time a water-driven woollen mill, hence the name Melin Llan. The water driven mills used to be quite common along the banks of the river as indicated by place names like Velindre, Melin Llan, and Cadle Mill. Cadle had a flourmill that was still operating in the 1920s. Some of the outbuilding survived and I remember seeing great big millstones propped up alongside one of these buildings.

E. Vyron Williams
2000

North Lodge

North Lodge is a two-storey building with another smaller one alongside. It is very quaint inside with small arched windows and a tiny grate at the far end, and is surrounded by beautiful rhododendron bushes, one being a rare scarlet colour. As for the lodge itself this has been left almost as it must have been when first built, with the modest addition of a square bay window to let more light into what was previously a rather dark lounge room. This same room once housed [*Sir John's*] butterflies and its walls were covered in net for the creatures to cling to.

Mrs. Nozicka remembers living there . . . and told me something of her life as a young girl. "My Aunt was a Miss Vaughan. She was the schoolteacher, Sunday School teacher, the organist at Church and very strict. When we attended school each girl was given a bonnet with a ribbon".

Jennie Bowen
aged 11, 1977
[Penllergaer Primary School project, including a recorded conversation with Phyllis Nozicka]

The original gate at North Lodge

Sir John . . . has a small cottage devoted to entomology, where he has an admirable collection of British lepidoptera, and where many of the species are reared from the larval state. To me this was specially interesting as it recalled my earlier days when the same pursuit had great fascination for me.

H. Honeywood D' Dombrain
The Gardener's Magazine
21st September 1895

Before Sir John passed away his daughter, Miss Gwendoline, still lived at the Big House and travelled around locally in a pony cart. She passed this way when she went to the village. She would stop outside and call "Vaughan! Vaughan!" and my father would go out to greet her. She often asked for a glass of water. We all knew it was just a pretext to stop and have a chat because she had only just left home!

Phyllis Nozicka
in conversation, 2003

Dear Mr. Maddox

[Extract from a letter written to A. J. Maddox on the 1st December 1950]

We are looking forward to digging into our chicken on Christmas Day. This brings to mind my recollections of the Christmas dinner given by Sir John and Lady Llewelyn [*at the end of the 19th century*] to the Sunday School children at the Sunday School. Everyone had to bring his own dinner plate, knife, fork and spoon, generally tied up in a large cloth or red handkerchief. Roast beef, turkey and pheasant and plenty of seasonable vegetables. The teacher and other helpers had to wait on us. The carving was done by Sir John and the butler and first footman. The plates now filled and ready, everything hot of course, – we had to stand and hear the Rev. T. P. Lewis say Grace. That over, we sat down and took up our 'tools' for demolition, when one of the boys would quietly pronounce 'The Hungry Boys' Grace' – 'Pitch in Boys, better belly bust than good food waste'. After dinner was cleared (by the way we had our plum pudding on the same plate) and everyone had packed his belongings again, we had the Christmas Tree and were also rewarded with an orange and a small bag of sweets. The whole affair ended about 4 p.m. then home again in time for tea, tired perhaps but happy . . .

W. T. Rosser

Below Stairs

My coal scuttle came from the Big House. Mother bought it at the sale in 1936 because she said she was the one who had filled it enough times. She was a parlour maid for Sir John. I think she went there when she was about eighteen and stayed for three or four years. It must have been about the time of the First World War. There is a lovely story about the time when Dad was working at the tin works and he was courting Mum. He had the afternoon off but Mum didn't. The weather that day was very nasty so they decided to stay indoors. Now, Sir John apparently was very fond of jigsaw

Annie and Reg Blackwell, 1921

puzzles and it seems he had just had a new one. Mum and Dad were in the Servant's Hall and they must have decided to do a jigsaw. So Mum went and found one from upstairs. They were involved with it when along came Sir John. "Annie, have you seen my new jigsaw puzzle?" This said in his high-pitched little voice that was getting quaverier as he got older. Of course there was consternation from them as they jumped to their feet explaining and started to pack it up. "No, no, no!" said he, "You continue. I'll have it later". I have always thought he must have been a very good, very easy and nice person to let those two young people just get on with it.

Nancy Pember
in conversation, 2005

We Move to Penllergare House (1927-1936)

A short time after Sir John's death in 1927 the Llewelyn family asked my father if he would go down to live in Penllergare House whilst they were deciding what they were going to do about it. Miss Gwendoline Llewelyn had bought a house in Swansea and now moved there. Sir Charles had been living, since his marriage, at Llysdinam, Newbridge-on-Wye and Mrs. Gladys Mount (Sir John's younger daughter) lived partly at Glasbury and partly in London with her two sons, Dick and Christopher.

We moved from Penplas to Penllergare House in 1927. This was to be a most wonderful childhood. We lived in a section of the house at the back and side. Of course all the indoor staff were no longer employed, but outside everything was maintained and the estate ran as usual. The keepers, gardeners and the woodsmen all continued with their work and so did the carpenter. The Llewelyn family had always looked after their staff very well and this continued while we were in residence. The gardens, lawns and conservatory were looked after by Mr. Edge with his two sons who all lived at the Gardener's House. Mr. Isaac Davies, the Head Keeper, and his team looked after the wildlife on the estate and organised any shooting parties. The band of woodsmen, who had worked on the estate for many years, continued to look after and care for the trees and shrubs, paths and water courses and kept them in good order. Each day Mrs. Regan came from her home in the village to do some general cleaning and Mr. Anthony came

Mrs. Richards and children outside the stables. Late 1920s

31

The Richards family in 1930

morning and evening to stoke the furnace and deal with wood for the fires. Mrs. Regan lived in a thatch-roofed house on the side of the road leading to Pontlliw and Mr. Anthony lived in the house adjoining the Miners' Welfare Hall in the village where he was caretaker. One day when Mrs. Regan was working at Penllergare a telephone call came through asking for her to go home as the house was on fire. One of the steam lorries had sent a spark from its fire and set the thatched roof alight.

Penllergare House was fully furnished the whole time we lived in it. A few items had been taken by Miss Llewelyn and Mrs. Mount, but everything else was in its place; beautiful furniture and furnishings, wonderful china and glass in showcases, pictures and artefacts of all kinds. The Library housed many hundreds of books, academic as well as more ordinary ones. We learnt so much, my brother and I, without knowing it. Of course we were not allowed to go on our own through the rooms, but it was marvellous to accompany my father when he went through to see all was well, to air rooms, to see that shutters were secure, to check on what needed to be done.

The carpenter's shop on the right in the backyard was a wonderful place for me when I was quite young. Mr. Jones was my friend of course and he often needed me to help him! One day I went with my father to see where Mr. Jones was replacing a floorboard upstairs and there were so many cockle shells in under the flooring. "How on earth had they got there?" I asked. My father explained that when the house was rebuilt a layer of shells had been set in between the ground floor and first floor to absorb any sound. It really was a quiet house.

The rooms contained all sorts of treasures. The Round Room was one of my favourites. It was the bedroom over the Library and was completely circular. The three windows were in the curve and the door, also curved, was opposite. The wallpaper in the room had roses on a trellis all around and although there was a door leading into the dressing-room and another door leading to a walk-in cupboard, neither of these was obvious and it was so beautifully furnished. The main staircase was a lovely construction of white marble, cantilevered with a curved rail and went along one curved wall of the inner hall; it started just outside the Dining Room door. The main passage upstairs was wide and had three large free-standing glass cases, in which were items brought back from travels abroad. One, I recall, contained things from China, another one items from Japan and the third from Egypt. There were also glass-fronted cabinets against the walls containing china and glass items and the carpet runners up the central part of the passage complemented what was all around.

Betty Richards
2005

Home Farm from the yard

Home Farm and Upper Lodge

I was born at Home Farm in 1925. It was Sir John's farm and my grandfather was running it for him as a farm bailiff. That is Thomas Cole, my grandfather on my father's side. My father lived at home, he had trained to be a blacksmith in Pembroke Dock but when he came up here he went to the colliery. He never worked on the farm at all. My grandfather moved around trying to find the best farm. He was always moving farms. He eventually landed up at Penllergare and they stayed for twenty-two years.

My parents met in Pembroke Dock. At that time the grandparents were between farms, because tenancies were only exchanged on Lady Day. So they lived next door to each other for a while. My mother hated this boy to begin with, he was always peeping over the wall and spying on her. Later she became ill and had to go to hospital and the nearest one was in Swansea, and the only people she knew there were these Coles – so she wrote and asked if she could stay with them. She used to walk every day from the farm to the hospital for treatment. Then she became the maid on the farm. They had two maids. Eventually she married Ben the farmer's son. His mother pushed them together. Her thinking being that once a maid, of course, she could carry on being a maid when she married. There would always be someone to look after 'her darling little boy'. He was spoiled rotten by his mother. You know when they used to put the threepenny bits in the Christmas pudding? She used to put her hand in and make sure they went into his portion. And being a farm, that hand was not always too clean . . . well, that's what my mother used to say. Eventually he went to work at Garngoch No. 3 mine as a fitter.

My grandmother died and my mother carried on a bit at the farm but I think she found out my grandfather 'cooked the books' and she wouldn't go along with it. My grandmother had obviously turned a blind eye. Mother said she wouldn't stay there and being so well thought of by the family at the Big House we were allowed to move to the Lodge. It was supposed to be temporary. Before that it had been convenient at the farm because it was nearer to the colliery and my father, being a fitter, was often fetched out in the middle of the night. It would have been nice to live in the village with people around. It was a bit lonely at the Lodge. I only had my dog Topsy for company. The Rees's were in the other Lodge, Nancy Rees was about ten or fifteen years older than me. It was a big difference at that age.

Home Farm

Miss Gwendoline went to Bryn Road after her father died in 1927. But she often came up by car to visit. She was my godmother (and a very good one as well) and she always brought a gift, a little something. When I wanted to go to Gowerton School, she told my mother to take me to a certain shop in Swansea (I think it was Kendals) to kit me out and she would pay the bill. I still have the bed she gave me, in the back bedroom, and the pram she gave me when I was a child. At the Coronation she gave me commemorative mugs and later on it was books . . . she even gave me her portable typewriter. My mother and she had become quite good friends.

The Barn at Home Farm

In the 1920s the top of the milk had to be taken down from Home Farm to the Big House by six o'clock in the morning for breakfast, and sometimes Miss Gwendoline would walk up to meet my mother. She would wait by the gate until my mother came down the lane. She thought a lot of my mother. She often came to the Lodge and gave my mother money, and things like that. She knew times were hard. Originally, Mrs. Freeman was going to be my godmother. I spent hours with the Freemans when I was a child and then one day Miss Gwendoline came up and said "I'm going to be her godmother" and Mrs. Freeman had to become the second one. She invited me to tea at Bryn Road many times – tea and buttered scones. During the war she went to Llandrindod Wells and I stayed with her there too. She invited me up for a fortnight so her maids could go on holiday. I was supposed to do a little bit of work . . . dust and things . . . but I was so scared I was going to break something. I was only fourteen. I had to make her bed too and help her get ready for bed at night. I had thirty shillings a week, can you imagine it! It was a lot of money at that time. Miss Gwendoline wasn't taking advantage. She gave me a holiday and the work was only about half an hour a day and she paid me for it too. Besides, I was out all day with the cook's daughter who was about the same age as me.

Arthur James Blackwell

Emma and the pigs

I was nursing when Miss Gwendoline died. After I trained I was at what later became the Miners' Convalescent Home in Langland, as it became a general hospital during the war. Someone was reading the *Evening Post* and said this lady, Gwendoline Dillwyn Llewelyn, had passed away. I burst out crying . . . in the ward . . . in front of all the patients. I was very upset.

After my mother died in 1949, Mrs. Bevan came down to the Lodge, and I said "I don't know how I'm going to clear this place up". Because, when we left the farm, so much furniture came with us, you could hardly move for the stuff. "Don't worry about cleaning, it is all going to be altered," Mrs. Bevan said. Rees Howells owned Upper Lodge first when the Bible College was at Penllergare. Then he sold off some of the properties and she bought the lodges. She enlarged the places and rented them out. She was a very shrewd business woman. I was sorry to leave Penllergare but times change and you have to strike out on your own, but a little bit of me still belongs there.

Betty Jenkins
in conversation, 2005

The Blackwells

My grandfather, Arthur James Blackwell, was born in 1872 and came to Penllergare in 1911 as under gamekeeper for Sir John. Originally the family came from Essex and the outskirts of London. He and my grandmother, Emma, were given Middle Lodge in which to live. Gradually over the years Emma found the scent of the azaleas too much for her in the spring. They were very highly perfumed and heady and really affected her, so they asked to be moved and were given the Twyn. They kept pigs, cows and chickens there and all the water came from a well. There used to be a large framed photograph of Emma feeding the pigs over the mantelpiece. I think it amused my grandmother to have this picture of her doing farming work but after she died, it disappeared. I don't think grandfather liked it very much. She died very young, in her early fifties, and grandfather married again, to Harriet, who was a widow. We lost touch with that side of the family after grandfather died. However, an extraordinary coincidence occurred because, quite by chance, last year we discovered Harriet's granddaughter Felicity lived in Canada only a few miles from where my daughter Mary lives and we all met up when my brother Jim and I went over to visit.

Arthur and Emma Blackwell had three children who grew up at Middle Lodge and then later at the Twyn. They were Ted, Kitty and Reg Blackwell. Our father Reg was the first telegraph boy in Gorseinon. He was very proud when he first got his uniform and he got a shilling extra for keeping his bicycle clean. They all went to the Board School in Penllergaer and so did my brother Jim and I.

Nancy Pember
in conversation, 2005

Private collection

Reg Blackwell, telegraph boy, (second from left) outside the post office in Penllergaer, c.1920

A Weekend Walk

My grandfather, William George Bryan, came to Penllergare as a gamekeeper in 1902 and lived at Tyle Du. His wife Jane was employed as a game cook at Penllergare House. They had four children. Years later I remember as a child going on a walk to Penllergare mansion with my mother, father and aunt. The caretaker shouted at us as we approached, but as soon as my mother was recognised we were given permission to continue on our way and told we could look around if we wanted. We went into the Big House and walked all over. We were amazed at the sheer size of the place, going from one room to another, on and on. I was very impressed but couldn't imagine why people needed so much space. The house was in a dreadful state of repair. Paint peeling. Wallpaper hanging off the walls. Very dirty and debris everywhere. We walked to the Waterfall and on the way back climbed up to the Walled Gardens. My father, who was a bit of a gardener, was very impressed with the size of one of the glasshouses. He said it was made out of teakwood and that was why it had lasted so long.

Private collection

William George Bryan

John Paddock
in conversation, 2005

Middle Lodge (Summer 1961 – Spring 1963)

During the months leading to the summer of 1961, my parents, Aneurin and Barbara Williams, my two sisters, Mair (five), Linda (four) and myself (eighteen months), had been living with my maternal grandparents at Ffordd y Brain, Fforesthall, together with my mother's five brothers and sisters. Unsurprisingly, my parents were eager to move out and set up their own home. When my grandmother's coalman, Joe Walters, who was at that time living at Middle Lodge with his wife, informed her that they were to vacate the house and return to live in Llansamlet, my parents decided to try and rent the house. My father contacted Owen John Bevan, an elderly man who lived on the square in Penllergaer and whose son, the owner of Middle Lodge, was an Anglican priest in England. The rent in 1961 was a pound a week which was thought to be expensive considering the remote location of the property.

On our arrival at the Woods, my father was struck by the inquisitiveness of the locals at the Old Inn in Penllergaer who wanted to know everything about us. Our neighbours at the time were Mr. and Mrs. James and their two sons in Upper Lodge

Private collection

Mair, Helen and Linda Williams

and Mr. Marlowe and his snakes at Lower Lodge. It was rumoured that Marlowe fed horsemeat to his snakes. My father remembers that a Polish man was living at the North Lodge.

The house, built in approximately 1840, was surprisingly well equipped for its time and location and had running water inside and a flush toilet outside. In 1961, the gate that for many years had been opened and closed by the tenants of the lodge was still in place outside the house. There was also a seat in front of the house and a small white fence. Linda remembers playing on a swing my father made on the tree outside and playing in a sandpit under the tree.

On entering the front door into a small passageway, a door on the right led into a large living room, with two windows and a fireplace on the back wall. A door straight ahead led into the kitchen that could also be

Middle Lodge – with Margaret Rees, c.1930

accessed by a back door from the left of the property. To the right of the house stood a large shed, which contained a petrol-fuelled generator, that supplied electricity. However, due to the prohibitively high cost of the fuel, our family mostly used oil lamps. There was a well approximately one hundred yards up the bank to the left of the house. Just before we left the Woods, tests carried out on the well's water showed that it was unfit for consumption. During the winter when the well froze, my parents used to take a tin bath down to the lake and carry water back to the house. The water was then boiled before it could be used for cooking, drinking and washing.

The house was accessible to vehicles and milk was delivered twice a week. Linda remembers the milkman bringing orange juice and Tunnock's chewy biscuits as a treat. Gas canisters were delivered by Briscoe and Son. Unfortunately, the coal merchants would deliver no less that a ton of coal at a time and as this was too expensive an outlay, we relied on burning logs from trees that my father cut down himself. The winter of 1962-63 was particularly cold and keeping the family warm was a constant challenge. Mair and Linda remember walking through the freezing woods to my grandparents' house and having their cold-numbed feet rubbed in front of the coal fire by our relatives.

One Saturday afternoon during that cold winter, my mother had taken the children to town and my father was in the house alone when a young boy about fourteen years old turned up at the house in a distressed state. He and his friend (from the Merrill family of Ffordd y Brain) had ventured out onto the frozen lake and had hacked a hole through the ice with an iron bar. Unfortunately he slipped through the ice and was holding on for his life while his friend ran for help. My father ran to the lake, saw the boy's head sticking out of the water and decided he had no choice but to try to get him out. He tentatively walked towards him, feeling the ice pinging under his feet. After lifting him from the icy water, he carried the shivering boy back to the house and tried

At the top of the Waterfall

to warm him in front of the fire. The police and an ambulance arrived and rushed the boy to Morriston Hospital. As his clothes were dripping wet, my father lent him his new navy coat to wear in the ambulance.

My sisters and I usually played outside the house but we sometimes ventured further into the woods, which at that time contained a much wider range of colours of rhododendron trees than exists there today. A favourite pastime of Mair and Linda was to take me for a walk and hide from me behind the trees. They would wait until I started howling and come to rescue me – great fun! On rare occasions our relatives came to visit and we would take a picnic down to the lake.

Immediately behind Middle Lodge stood an imposing oak tree that features in the sad story related by locals, of a young man who lived at the lodge during the 1920s. It seems that the Dillwyn Llewelyn family took a particular interest in the boy who was very bright, and acted as mentors by encouraging him to study for entrance to medical school. Unfortunately he failed his exams and in his desperation, hanged himself on this tree. My father and others were convinced that the lodge was haunted and on several occasions heard footsteps walking up the stairs in the middle of the night. Mair remembers being terrified by the ghost and spent many nights hiding under the bedclothes.

Due to a combination of the ghost, the inconvenience and the severity of the winter of 1963, we were relieved to leave the Woods and move to an ordinary house in an ordinary street. Since leaving Middle Lodge, we have returned several times over the years and each time we have witnessed the gradual disappearance of the house into the undergrowth. By now, it seems strange to think that this neglected and abandoned place, that is now considered to be worthy of interest, was once our home.

Helen Williams
July 2005

Keeper's Lodge

This was where the Dillwyn Llewelyn's head gamekeeper lived when the place was run as a country estate. The Pheasantry was in the field next to the house where they had the rearing pens. There are still pheasants to be seen wandering about today. In the 1930s there was a tennis court here and the locals came here to play. The cottage is bigger than it looks, seven rooms in all, stone built and solid; and with the best views out anyone could wish. You can see everything that is going on from up here.

I've lived up here for forty years. I saw this advert in the paper that it was for sale, I was living in Birmingham at the time, so my father Patsy Power came here first. Although we are of Irish descent, the family had previously lived in Fforestfach, so we knew this area very well. At first there was some confusion about the name. The deeds said one thing and the locals called it something else. So I went to the post office in Gorseinon and asked them. Y Bwthyn they said. Well, that was alright for me . . . then everyone started calling it Keeper's Lodge again!

Tyrone Power
in conversation, 2006

Nydfwch

The precise meaning and derivation of the place-name remains obscure but the location survives today in Graig Neddfwch Wood which reaches a height of 91 metres (300 feet) and overlooks the now reinstated Lower Lake. The origins of Nydfwch date from at least the late thirteenth century and it remained an independent entity for over four hundred and fifty years before it became integrated with Penllergare. In 1750 the heiress of Nydfwch, Jane Mathews (1728-58), married Gryffydd Price (1718-87) the heir to Penllergare.

There is no conclusive evidence as to when the house was demolished although the property may still have been standing in 1822. The majority of the land became part of Brynrhos Farm and the other fifty acres of Nydfwch were converted into Lower Lake in the late 1830s, itself part of a wholesale programme of change initiated by John Dillwyn Llewelyn.

No pictorial representation of the house exists and apart from the 1670 hearth tax assessment, which lists Henry Mathews liable for tax on five hearths and one in the dairy, the only other evidence that survives is a probate inventory of 29th March 1730. This room by room survey reveals a two-storey property comprising at least ten rooms as follows: hall; chamber over the hall; middle chamber and nursery; chamber over the

Jennie Eyers

View towards Llangyfelach from Craig Nydfwch Wood

39

porch; the best chamber; the chamber over the kitchen; the upper kitchen; the garret and the store room.

It seems reasonable to deduce, that as well as increasing its area from a modest twenty-two acres to ninety-four, the opportunity was also taken to rebuild Brynrhos farmhouse in the 1820s or early 1830s. With the exception of Bryndafydd Fawr (which has been modernised in recent years) compared with other farmhouses in the vicinity, such as Parc Mawr and the ruined Glynsilling and Bryndafydd Fach, Brynrhos is uncharacteristically large. It is therefore suggested that in looking at Brynrhos today one is perceiving (at least in terms of stones and mortar) the former Nydfwch mansion, though whether it is architecturally and aesthetically similar is doubtful.

Jeff Childs, MA
Extracts from "In Search of Nydfwch"
(*Gower*, Vol. 51. 2000)

Nydfwch and Brynrhos

I think some of the materials from the old manor house of Nydfwch were used at Brynrhos. People used to do that centuries ago, didn't they? Nothing was wasted. It was an early form of recycling. If a place was abandoned and in ruins then the stone and timber would be useful somewhere else. They certainly did not have to transport it far as Brynrhos Farm is only a field or two away. If you went up into the roof space at the farm and looked at the beams and joists it was obvious they had been used before because they didn't match. There were signs of nail holes and on the stairs the mortise and tenons didn't match either. There were also signs of the re-use of timbers in the cellar. Someone said that the huge beams in the cowshed were salvaged from the sailing ships that came into the port at Swansea.

Jennifer Cloke

River Llan in autumn

Of course there is nothing left of Nydfwch now except some stones lying about and a few mounds. When I was younger there were masses of snowdrops in the spring which is an obvious sign there had been human habitation there once. Then further over towards Nydfwch woodland was a field that was a carpet of bluebells in the spring. We called it the Blue Field. It was beautiful.

Jeffrey Phillips
in conversation, 2005

Jeffrey Phillips

Lower Lodge in the 1960s

Green Days and Blue Days
(My boyhood at Penllergare)

I was born at Lower Lodge, the Cadle Mill entrance to Penllergare, in March 1926. One of my first memories is looking out of my bedroom window some four years later and instead of seeing the field which was between our back yard and the river (the Afon Llan) there was a sheet of water. The river was in flood. I little realised then what influence that river, and water generally, would have on the next ten years of my life.

There was no piped water to the Lodge. We had to carry all drinking water from a well in Cadle Mill and as soon as I was old enough, about the age of seven, I had to help my older sister and brother. We had a couple of casks which collected rain water from the roof for domestic use but there were some dry summers when this supply ran out and I had to help Father carry water from the river. This was no easy task, the field sloped and the river being shallow and the bank dry you could easily slip into the water.

The river had another big influence on our life. It was the boundary between two councils. The left bank (Cadle Mill) came under Swansea Town Council which was not a city in those days. Our lodge being on the right bank came under Loughor Urban District Council. Children living in Cadle Mill went to school at Fforestfach which was only about fifteen minutes' walk away. I and my sister, and brother before me, had to go to Penllergaer School which was about one and a half miles and all up hill. This was not at all funny on a winter's day when there was no penny for the bus.

The river did, however, have its good side. It was very much part of my playground on the estate. There were only two children of my age in Cadle Mill, Joyce Taylor and Haydn Williams, and we would spend hours during the school holidays exploring Penllergare. We would often walk to near the Big House, then down the steps and along the path to the Boathouse. Here we would sit with our bag of crisps and pretend we were on a fishing trip and a picnic. Then on to Lower Lake and to the dam waterfall and cross at the base. There were stepping stones but one slip and it was wet feet. Then homewards along the left bank looking for duck eggs and emerge at Cadle Mill Farm.

Some special events stand out in my memory and one was the annual Boxing Day Hunt. The meet was right outside our lodge, so I had a ringside seat. It was noisy and colourful and the Town Clerk of Swansea, Mr. Lancoath,

Jeffrey Phillips

Lower Lodge in the 1960s

41

The Gun Room, in the stable block where William Edge and his family lived for a time in the 1930s

I think he was Master of the Hunt, changed into his hunting clothes in our front room. He was always very polite to mother and used to give her a half crown.

Finally, there are two more memories connected with water. In 1937 the Bible College of Wales leased the Big House; I never remember anyone calling it the mansion. The head of the college was the Rev. Rees Howells and he used to visit the students at the Big House on a regular basis. The following year two relatives (I think they were nephews) of the ex-Emperor of Ethiopia, Haile Selassie, arrived as students and he, who was now living in the UK, started visiting the Big House with the Rev. Howells. We noticed that they would park the car between the main road and our lodge and walk up the drive. One day they were returning from such a visit when there was a thunderstorm and torrential rain. They ran for shelter onto our porch. Mother immediately invited them in and offered them a cup of tea; the teapot was always on the hob. The Rev. and Mother tried to get some sort of conversation going but the ex-Emperor hardly said a word. He seemed puzzled by the number of doors in our living room. There were five doors and I suppose, looking back, that is unusual. Fortunately the rain soon eased and they departed with handshakes all round. When I returned to school and told the story no one believed me.

Then there was an outing on the Lower Lake, which could have ended in tragedy. It was late December 1939 and very cold. My brother Ivor, then twenty years of age, knew the Lake was frozen and suggested that we see if we could get to the island which is about two thirds of the way across from the west bank. I collected my friend Haydn and off we went. All went well until we were within striking distance of the island when there were cracks in the ice. We didn't realise then that was probably where the Afon Llan flowed into the Lake. I noticed Ivor had gone very pale. He said we had to get back as fast as possible and to spread out as we went. Immediately Haydn fell and wearing short trousers cut his knee. Ivor went to his aid and told me to hurry back. Now there were cracks appearing around us all the time. When I reached the bank I was so exhausted I could hardly scramble up it. I was freezing cold and anxious and it seemed an age before the others made it back to the bank too. I have never since been anywhere near ice.

It was just about the end of my boyhood at Penllergare. Two months later mother died. Four months after that I left school and started my first job. Nine months further on I looked out of my bedroom window at the Lodge for the last time. It was goodbye to the Afon Llan. We were moving to Fforestfach to a house with running water and electricity and – a fish and chip shop next door!

Victor Webb
2006

The Coach House

My grandfather's name was Frank Brown and he was caretaker at Penllergare. The Second World War was over and my parents had nowhere to live, and because my grandfather had a house in Gorseinon, my parents were given permission to live in the coach house, which was actually joined onto the back of the Big House. My grandfather died in 1950 and so we had to leave and Mr. Reynish took over as caretaker.

Inside the mansion, the huge marble staircase was a beautiful feature of the hallway but had a little chip out of the middle of every step. We understood that when the Americans were there during the war they had made the marks by dragging heavy office furniture down the stairs. My mother had teenage brothers who would bring lots of girlfriends to the estate. The billiards room was still intact when we lived there and was used by my family. I can remember the dumb waiter and the cellars, where I used to play with my brother, who was twenty months older than me. We both remember the garage with the inspection pits very well because it was our play area. Years ago I expect the carriages were kept there and then Sir John's car. Above the pits my uncles had tied some ropes and we used to swing across them.

We frequently used the two estate entrances nearest to the Big House. If we were going to get milk in the morning from Mrs. Bevan, who had the shop next door to the Old Inn, we would use the North Entrance and pass Phyllis Nozicka's North Lodge. Olaf, her husband, was very big and handsome and they often came out to speak to us if they saw us passing by. If we were going to catch the bus to Gorseinon, we would use the Melin Llan entrance. The main drive from the south we hardly ever used. However, on one occasion I remember us all coming home from Swansea on the bus, and at Cadle there was another bus on fire. We got off there because the road was blocked, and walked past the little cottages up the drive to the Big House. My mother said "never again" as she found it too far.

Beryl Brain
2004

The Lamb and Flag

At the beginning of the twentieth century the Penllergare grounds were opened to the public on the 1st May and people came from everywhere to walk through and admire the flowers. I walked up the drive from Cadle where I lived and would come out at Penllergaer village. It was

Private collection

Cadle: the Lamb and Flag on the left

Watercolour by D. R. Williams (1999) based on the previous photograph. The cottages in the centre were reputedly designed by Emma Dillwyn Llewelyn

something we looked forward to every year smelling those wonderful azaleas and seeing all the beautiful colours.

I was born at the Lamb and Flag ninety-four years ago, although it wasn't a public house when we lived there, it was just 3 Cadle Cottages. Originally it was thatched and at some time it became an inn and it had quite a big cellar where they stored the ale. Someone told me Sir John closed it down because there was too much drunkenness and fighting going on at the entrance to his estate. The cottages all belonged to him anyway, so he was within his rights. I was told I always had to curtsey when Sir John went by in his car, someone would be driving it for him, and if he saw me he gave me a little wave. There were three bedrooms upstairs and below was a parlour, middle room and a smaller place where we did the washing. All the cooking and eating took place in the middle room. We were a large family.

When I was about eight years old Sir John would come down in a pony trap to fetch my father for the shoots. They needed beaters and my father always went to help. He would be given two rabbits and two pheasants, which pleased him a lot. I don't know if he got any money as well. Sir John was very elderly at this time, very hunched up, but got around in his pony cart. One of the sons at the Big House, or it might have been a grandson, had a bicycle and he came very fast down the Drive and would whisk past me. I always thought he would be in Swansea by the time I walked another two yards!

My father was killed in an accident at Tirdonkin Colliery. It was the same year Sir John died. The pit was on estate land and everyone knew it was unsafe. After my father and the others died they closed the pit down but we were allowed to stay on in the house. Many years later the people at the Big House offered to sell it to my mother for a nominal sum.

Elizabeth Williams (née Taylor)
in conversation, 2003

My mother, Gladys, was one of eleven children who grew up at the Lamb and Flag. Apparently, early in the twentieth century, the thatch was set alight by a firework and completely destroyed. When the estate people came to estimate the repair my grandmother, Ellen Taylor, said she didn't want thatch again, she wanted a proper roof! Later, during the war, many of our relations came out from Swansea to stay here during the 'three day blitz'. There were several families in every room, including the garage. It is only a small place but my mother couldn't turn anyone away, she was that sort of person.

June Phillips
in conversation, 2006

Sunday School

After Sir John died, Mrs. Mount often came with Dick and Christopher to spend the day at Penllergare. They usually brought a hamper of food, which her cook had prepared. In those days I think Dick liked fishing and, of course, the river at Penllergare was very good for trout. Sir Charles and Lady Llewelyn would come and perhaps stay a few nights when they would bring with them a cook and a maid. Sir Charles would organise a shoot. Lady Llewelyn always came during the summer to present prizes to members of the Sunday School.

The parkland at Penllergare between the North Lodge, the Home Farm and up to the Iron Gate on the Swansea Road often had visitors on Sunday School outings from around the district. Gorseinon held their Sunday School outing quite often in the park and St. Gabriel's Church in Swansea came most years. The woods beyond the parkland were a private place and were not available to the general public. This was so for the whole time that we were living at Penllergare House from 1927 until the end of 1936.

I recall a couple of occasions when 'our gang' acted as 'keepers of that privacy'. When we knew that an outing was happening we would sit on the wall by the kissing gate leading to the Tennis Garden and if any children came to the gate we told them about all these frightening wild animals that roamed the woods! We said there were lions, tigers and wolves who particularly liked eating children because they tasted so sweet! The children quickly ran back to safety. What terrible children we must have been!

Quarry Bridge in winter 2005

Betty Richards
2005

John Dillwyn Llewelyn (1810–1882)

John Dillwyn Llewelyn was the eldest son and second child of Lewis Weston Dillwyn and his wife Mary (née Adams, the illegitimate daughter of Colonel John Llewelyn). John inherited two estates from his maternal grandfather (Ynysygerwyn in the Neath Valley and Penllergare four miles north of Swansea) and, on coming of age, and according to instructions in the Colonel's will, added the name of Llewelyn to his own.

Although he was educated at home he matriculated in 1827 and went up to Oriel College, Oxford the following year. He was elected a fellow of the Linnean Society in 1831 and of the Royal Society in 1832.

In 1833 John married Emma Thomasina Talbot, the youngest daughter of Thomas Mansel Talbot and Lady Mary Lucy (née Strangways) of Margam and Penrice. Significantly, Emma was first cousin to the pioneer photographer Henry Fox Talbot. The newly-weds set up home at Penllergare. During the honeymoon and early days of the marriage, the house underwent considerable alteration and refurbishment and there was much improvement, in design and layout, to the gardens and surrounding parkland.

John and Emma eventually had seven children, six of whom survived into adulthood. The eldest was a daughter Thereza (1834-1926), their son and heir was John Talbot (1836-1927) known during his young life as 'Johnny'; then followed Emma Charlotte (1837-1928), William Mansel (1838-1866) called 'Willy' by the family, Sybella (1842) who died in infancy, Elinor (1844-1887) and Lucy (1846-1920).

Although John Dillwyn Llewelyn was a man of independent means, his interests and preoccupations were eclectic. He became actively involved with local affairs. He qualified as a magistrate and was made High Sheriff of the County of Glamorgan. He was a noted philanthropist, giving both time and money to many good causes, sitting on committees and acting as benefactor to local schools and hospitals. For his employees, who were not accommodated on the estate, he had cottages built, (reputedly designed by Emma) near to his newly endowed Chapel of Ease, later to become St. David's parish church, at Cors Eynon. With his brother Lewis and brother-in-law Matthew Moggridge, in 1843 he became an active participant in aiding Captain Napier and the police to quell a local Rebecca Riot at the Bargoed tollgate, Pontardulais. After threats of a French invasion in the mid-nineteenth century John supported and trained his own militia, the 5th Company Glamorgan Rifle Volunteers (founded 12th October 1859) until they were disbanded some fourteen years later. He gave land in Cockett for the building of Cottage Homes in an effort to save poor families from the workhouse and also gave a forty-two acre holding known as Knap Llwyd near Morriston to the local people as a public park (now called Parc Llewelyn).

John Dillwyn Llewelyn was a committed family man who, though not a prolific diarist like his father, kept the occasional journal, wrote accounts of local events, papers for the Royal Institution of South Wales, and frequent letters to the family, particularly his wife, when away from home. For his children he wrote and illustrated stories, often of a chivalric nature and set in fictitious but instantly recognisable local places.

Throughout his life he was intensely interested in horticulture, botany and arboriculture and the grounds of Penllergare became renowned for their innovative landscape design in the then fashionable 'picturesque' style. John Dillwyn Llewelyn exploited the natural beauty of the site and created an ornamental park of great variation and mood that he stocked with a rich assortment of trees and shrubs, native and exotic plants. He was particularly fond of orchids and in the middle of the Walled Gardens he created his unique orchideous house, possibly the first designed one of its kind in the British Isles. Since 1835 he had developed an increasing interest in the cultivation and display of orchids and in 1836 he wrote to his father:

"The Stove [*heated glasshouse*] has a great promise . . . all know that. The back of the stove which I had left unfinished . . . I have now determined on glazing – It will be only small and entirely given up to Orchis – 100 degrees of heat and an atmosphere saturated with water, is the enjoyment I promise myself and my pets – I intend them to flower there and to rest after the exertion in a dryer and cooler place".

An article he wrote for the first edition of the *Journal of the Horticultural Society* (1846) survives as evidence of the design, together with a ground and elevation plan and a drawing of the rockwork cascade.

Like many gentry families of the period the Dillwyn Llewelyns had a lively interest in natural history and the emerging sciences. John was a gifted amateur scientist and a member of the RISW. With his fervent interest in scientific invention, he became involved, with the engineer Benjamin Hill of Clydach, in the design of an electrically-powered boat that had its first public demonstration on the lake at Penllergare when the British Association for the Advancement of Science met in Swansea in 1848. He also assisted Sir Charles Wheatstone with experiments of electrical underwater telegraphy off Mumbles Head and with the ringing of an electric bell between the Lodge and the dining room at Sketty Hall.

His interest in astronomy led to the building of an equatorial observatory (the second only in Wales) adjacent to the mansion. The foundation stone was laid in 1851 by his daughter Thereza, accompanied by her sisters Emma Charlotte and Elinor. John was elected a fellow of the Royal Astronomical Society the same year. It was from the Observatory that father and daughter took one of the first photographs of the moon.

It is perhaps as a photographer that John Dillwyn Llewelyn is now best remembered. Initially influenced by Henry Fox Talbot he became enthusiastic and skilful and Penllergare was pivotal in providing an infinite variety of subjects for his camera. Eventually John was recognised as one of the foremost British pioneer photographers.

A founder Council Member of the Photographic Society of London (now the Royal Photographic Society), he exhibited at all their early exhibitions and at Paris in 1855, winning a Silver Medal. He has left a large archive of material, principally to be found in Swansea Museum, the National Library of Wales and the National Museums of Wales, that is considered central to the development and spirit of photography. His work includes pictures taken on family visits and tours of the British Isles; but it is the photographs he took of the landscape and gardens at Penllergare and of his young growing family that possibly remain his most evocative, showing a particular passion for his own private world.

His last years were plagued by ill health. The asthma he suffered from for most of his life grew worse. He and Emma went to live in London, eventually buying Atherton Grange in Wimbledon in 1879. It was here that Emma died in 1881 and John survived her by only sixteen months, dying in 1882. Both in turn were brought back to Wales and buried in the churchyard of St. David's, Penllergaer.

Jennie Eyers
2003
Based on research by
Richard Morris, M.Phil, FRPS

Oak trees. Photograph by John Dillwyn Llewelyn, c.1850

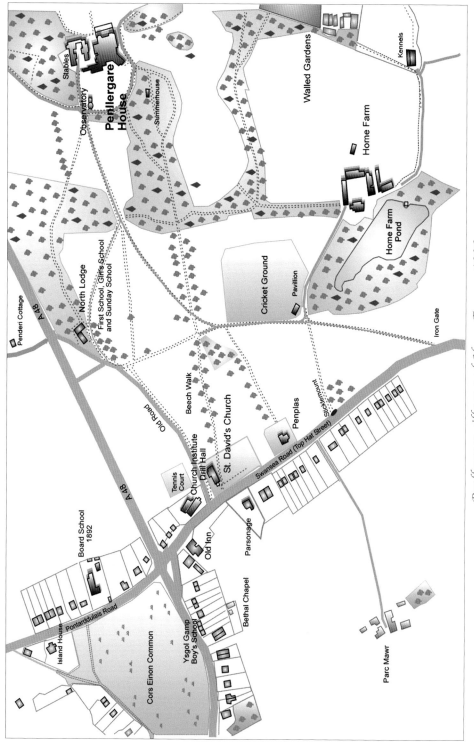

Penllergaer village and Home Farm, c.1936

The Walled Gardens. Although damaged in places, much of the existing structure is capable of being repaired and the gardens brought back to life

Chris Cray

The Gardens and Gardeners

Snowdrops

The winters breath was chill and rude
The ground with icy covering strewed
Was chill and wan,
As Flora ventured sadly forth
Amid the tempests of the north
Bereaved and lone.

Her children's favourite haunts she sought
But e'en on sunniest banks were nought
But frozen tombs,
Till rising welcome to her view
She spied amid the ice a few
Pale snowdrop blooms.

She stooped to kiss the drooping bells
That lay like some pale pearly shells
On oceans shore,
And breathing in a fond caress
Began to thaw the icy dress
That winter wore.

She breathed and see the icy chain
Which marked the tyrants winter reign
Is broken now,
The shroud of sleet dissolves away
And shining leaves their charm display
Beneath the snow.

John Dillwyn Llewelyn
1843

My dear Mamma

[Extract from a letter to her mother, Lady Mary Cole]

As I suppose Mary is gone from you I must write you a separate account of my nursery – we are all going on well now, tho' their colds hang about the children so as to hinder their leaving the nursery which is always a great deprivation to their Papa. This lovely weather is just what I could wish for and I get out – and accomplish a bit of gardening now & then as well as wading through the mud & swamps in the valley to see John's great works – he is so busy now, planting Ghent azaleas, hemlock spruces, deciduous

Inside the Orchideous House, 1846.
Watercolour by George Delamotte

cypresses, yews, laburnums, & Norway maples & Weymouth pines down by the Lago Maggiore [*their name for Lower Lake*] – Also making a boat house to the Upper Lake in the style of the chalet in the 'Canadian Scenery' which I daresay you remember and subjoining a rough aviary to break one side, by way of beginning a sort of zoological gardens (of birds) which he always had a hankering after. I heard a very good account of dear Mrs. Dillwyn a few days ago but have seen nobody lately except Mrs. Lewis Dillwyn who came over for five minutes the other day – Fanny was to be at Sketty to stay, this week. We have got some beautiful little daffodils which were brought in bud yesterday & are all blown out in the water today. The hares crop all my *Cunae* anemonies in front except where I have wires.

Emma Thomasina Dillwyn Llewelyn
31st December 1841

My dear Father

[Extract from a letter to his father, Lewis Weston Dillwyn]

. . . I am getting again deeply into all my old pursuits, experiments horticultural and agricultural – in the garden especially busy. The Orchid House in especial delights me and the plants in the damp atmosphere of the fall seem to forget their captivity and spread out their roots in all directions to drink the misty air.

John Dillwyn Llewelyn
November 1843

Some Account of an Orchideous House, constructed at Penllergare, South Wales. By J. D. Llewelyn, Esq., F.H.S.

The account by Schomburgk of the splendid vegetation which borders the cataracts of tropical rivers gave me the first idea of trying this experiment. I was delighted with the beautiful picture which his words convey, and thought it might be better represented than is usual by stoves of this country.

With this in view I began to work, and added the rock-work to a house already in use for the cultivation of orchideous plants. The water for the supply of the cascade is conducted to the top of the house by means of a pipe communicating with a pond at a higher level *[Home Farm pond]*. This pipe is warmed by passing through a single coil through the boiler, and terminates at the top of the rock-work, where it pours a constant supply of water over three projecting irregular steps of rough stone, each of which catches the falling stream, dividing it into many smaller rills and increasing the quantity of misty spray. At the bottom the whole of the water is received into the pool which occupies the centre of the floor of the stove, where it widens out into an aquarium ornamented with a little island overgrown like the rock-work with Orchidae, ferns and lycopods.

Plants that are grown in this manner have a wild luxuriance about them that is unknown to the specimens cultivated in the ordinary manner, and to myself they are exceedingly attractive, more resembling what one fancies them in their native forests – true air plants, depending for their subsistence on the humid atmosphere alone.

It must be remembered that this plan may be added to any existing stove, and that the sole expense will be for the pipe to conduct the stream, and for the labour of the carriage and arrangement of the rock-work. A small quantity of water is sufficient, and this, after passing through the stove, might be conveniently used for garden purposes.

Adapted from an article by John Dillwyn Llewelyn
28th October 1845
Published in *The Journal of the Horticultural Society*, Volume 1, 1846

Private collection

Chris Cray

Watercolour by Amy Dillwyn. One hundred and fifty years apart, the painting and the photograph are possibly of the same place and both could depict the sycamore that Thereza writes about in her diary

Interior of the Orchid House, c.1855.
Photograph by John Dillwyn Llewelyn

Thereza's Diary

. . . Grandmama told me about Penllergare in former days, when there was a road and a row of trees between the house and the valley. The sycamore tree was one and on the south side of it there was a gap which allowed the valley to be seen from the house. In Mr. Price's (counsellor) time, he had a summerhouse there, where he could do business. Then there was a garden in terraces all down the steep bank to the river, walls were built in several places, to keep the bank up, they remain at present mostly. Grandmama had first only the border under the upper wall (close to the sycamore) . . . After that she got the piece of ground between the next walls for her own, and that is what we called the rockwork garden. Below that it was all kitchen garden. The road was kept private, but an old woman about ninety years old had the privilege of passing that way, on Sundays, when she used to ride to Nydfwch, then to Llangyfelach to church. The place is certainly wonderfully changed since then!

Thereza Dillwyn Llewelyn
10th August 1856

The Upper Valley

As the house is neared the scenery becomes still grander. The valley narrows and deepens and the drive for some distance runs close to the edge of a precipice, with only a frail rustic wooden rail between the road and it for protection; or, what is more reasonable, to mark the edge of the cliff, which descends perpendicularly 100 feet or more below the road. The view from this point, looking to the right over the tops of trees and down to the bottom of the glen, is charming. The ground from the foot of the precipice sweeps boldly down to the river, and then rises rapidly to a great height on the opposite side, completely shutting in the view. The view from the left side of the road is hemmed in by the rock out of which it is cut, and the rising ground above it. Advantage has been taken of the narrowness of the valley here to make a lake by throwing a bank across it and damming the stream. The lake is beautifully situated and its surface along the margin is covered with different kinds of water lilies, while the steep banks on all sides are wooded down to the water's edge. In the middle of the bank, at the lowest end of the lake, there is a strong bulwark composed of large blocks of stone which forms the resisting power to the heavy weight

Rockwork Walk. Mid 1850s
Photograph by John Dillwyn Llewelyn

of water at a point where the lake forms a cascade, which leaps boldly over a fall of 18 feet, and then the river assumes its natural course down the valley till it is again interrupted where it forms another lake of greater dimensions. Both lakes are well stocked with trout, which affords great sport to Mr. Llewelyn and his friends from boats during the fishing season. From this point the drive continues to rise gradually till it emerges in front of the mansion on a small open plateau, which is neatly laid out in shrubberies, flowerbeds and plots of well-kept short grass. Here the ground immediately to the right descends to the lake, and for some distance past the east side of the house. Shady winding walks lead from the mansion down to the lake, and along its side nearest the house, past the cascade, and down the right side of the stream for a great distance till it is

Chris Cray

Steps to the Walled Gardens

crossed by a bridge, where the walks diverge into the woods and ascend the opposite bank. *Osmunda regalis* and other British ferns in great variety grow luxuriantly in every available spot, and fringe the banks and sides of the stream abundantly.

Andrew Pettigrew
The Journal of Horticulture and Cottage Gardener
June/July 1886

Orchids

Penllergare has had one advantage which many places have not possessed for the late Mr. Llewelyn, father of the present owner, was a keen horticulturalist and I believe was one of the very first who took up the cultivation of orchids and in conjunction with Mr. Bateman sent out collectors to the East Indies and other places for the obtaining and sending home those floral treasures of that widely-extended and most varied family which have now become so much the rage amongst horticulturalists, and in truth he could have had but little idea of the extent to which this cultivation would attain, or of the grand species which the later half of the present century have brought to our gardens from all parts of the world.

H. Honeywood D' Dombrain
The Gardener's Magazine
21st September 1895

Rhododendrons

The immense quantities of rhododendrons, species and hybrids, that are grown here form one of the principal features of the place. Rhododendrons are growing everywhere about the grounds – in shrubberies, woods, and in clumps on the open lawn, with a luxuriance to be met with only in a few places favoured by soil and climate. Mr. Llewelyn and his father before him have taken great interest in the cultivation and introduction of new species and varieties of rhododendrons that will stand the climate of Penllergare and their efforts in this, as evidenced by the fine collections, have been crowned with no small degree of success. Thousands of seedlings from the best species and varieties are raised annually in boxes and planted out in nursery lines in succession, where they remain until they are large enough to be planted permanently in favourable situations in the woods or elsewhere. The seeds are sown early in spring and the boxes placed in a vinery for the seeds to germinate, which they do freely to judge from the boxes I saw covered with young plants as thickly as if it had been mustard and cress. The varieties consisted of the choicest kinds in cultivation, amongst which I observed the following: *R. viviani, R. eximium, R. hodgsonii, R. barbatum, R. fulgens, R. cinnabarinum, R. ciliatum, R. thomsonii, R. fortunei, R. arboreum, R. calophytum* and many others. In passing I may say the rhododendrons at the time of my visit were in full flower. I am sorry, however, that time did not permit of my noting the names and giving the dimensions of some of the adult plants which are growing here so plentifully.

Andrew Pettigrew
The Journal of Horticulture and Cottage Gardener
June/July 1886

A Paradise

The real glory of Penllergare consists of its truly magnificent grounds, and its rare and beautiful plants which add a superabundance of attractions to a spot already marked by nature for special favours.

The South Wales Daily News
20th August 1910

Grandfather's Footsteps

My family was firmly entwined with Penllergare and the Dillwyn Llewelyns for over twenty years in the middle of the 19th century. Researching my family history I discovered my great, great grandfather, John Nunns, was John Dillwyn Llewelyn's Head Gardener.

He was at Penllergare at a time when the landscape and gardens were going through fundamental redevelopment and he must have been instrumental in its implementation. He lived in the Gardener's House and the Walled Gardens would have been his domain. The Walled Gardens supplied all the fruit and vegetables for those who lived and worked at the Big House and he would also have grown and nurtured the small trees, shrubs and flowers for planting in the gardens and the exhibits for all the horticultural shows they entered.

Chris Cray

Rhododendron

John Nunns was baptised on 24th December 1828 and came from a long line of gardeners. His father, William, rented property and land

Rhododendrons

from the Earl of Macclesfield in the early nineteenth century and built up a nursery and seedsman business in Leek. William also rented off plots of land in Leek as 'allotments' (known as Nunns Gardens) and to this day there are two streets in Leek known as Garden Street and Nunns Street. In 1851, his son John, carrying on the family tradition, was 'second gardener' aged twenty-two at Westbury on Trym, Bristol and some time between then and 1861 he became Head Gardener at Penllergare. He married Elizabeth King who came from Devon. Their son, William King Nunns was born on 15th February 1864 and his birth certificate describes John as the 'Master Gardener at Penllergare'. Sadly, Elizabeth died aged forty-two from Bright's Disease and is buried in the cemetery of St. David's Church. Three years later John married Sarah, Elizabeth's younger sister.

Eventually, when Emma and John Dillwyn Llewelyn moved to Atherton Grange in Wimbledon (leaving their son John Talbot D.L. in charge at Penllergare) they could not bear to be parted from their Head Gardener, so the Nunns family went with them. There they remained, continuing to live in Wimbledon in retirement, after the deaths of their employers.

When I visited Penllergare it was particularly magical knowing that I was walking in my great, great grandfather's footsteps, seeing what he would have seen and walking where he would have walked. It was an emotional moment but I felt very much at ease, it was almost like 'a coming home'. Paradoxically, my father and grandfather enjoyed a nice neat garden but HATED GARDENING!

Linda Tully (née Nunns)
2005

The Orchid House and Vineries

After leaving the Melon Ground with its many objects of interest, we were shown through the forcing and plant house. The first of these, a lean-to greenhouse, was furnished with a good selection of tuberous begonias, vallotas, pelargoniums and a choice collection of cool orchids. The roof was partly covered by a large plant of *Lapageria alba*, which grows vigorously and flowers freely, the flowers lasting for a long time in perfection before fading. Next to this is an Orchid House, which contains a rich collection of well-grown plants, clean and healthy. Mr. Llewelyn is a good orchidist, and perhaps it would not be too much to say that he inherits his love for them from his late father, who was deeply interested in their introduction and cultivation, that he and another gentleman employed a collector of orchids between them long before *Orchideae* became so common in this country.

The next range consists of three lean-to vineries each about fifty feet in length. The first of these was filled with a Black Hamburgh Vine some eighty years old, it is planted in an inside border and produces heavy crops of medium-sized bunches yearly. The second division is planted with Lady Downe's Seedling and Black Hamburgh, which were carrying heavy crops of large bunches. The third division is planted with late varieties, which prolong the supply of grapes to the end of March. The vines in all the divisions were clean and healthy, and showed signs of good culture throughout.

Andrew Pettigrew
The Journal of Horticulture and Cottage Gardener
June/July 1886

Chris Cray

Outside the Walled Gardens

Rhododendrons at Penllergare, Swansea

From the middle of January to the middle of February, 1917, the weather in South Wales was exceptionally severe, and during most of that time the easterly wind blew a blizzard, with much snow and frost, which attained a maximum of twenty-eight degrees early in February. Many conifers were scorched quite brown on the eastern side, many semi-hardy or tender shrubs such as veronicas, myrtles and some bamboos were killed or severely injured, but the rhododendrons and azaleas came through the winter far better than I expected.

The foliage of some of the more exposed plants was torn off by the violence of the wind, but the actual injury by frost to the plants was certainly less than was the case in November, 1893, when the sap and young wood was less matured than it was in January, 1917.

My plants of *Rhododendron grande* have suffered, though I think they will recover, while such species as *barbatum, thomsonii, ochraceum, campanulatum, griffithianum, roylei, campylocarpum, falconeri, hodgsonii* and *cinnabarinum* are uninjured and most of them are showing a very fair average of bloom for 1918. No azalea seems to be any the worse, still I cannot help hoping we may not be subjected to so sharp a test again in this coming spring.

John T. D. Llewelyn
14th December 1917
The Rhododendron Society Notes, Volume 1, Part 3

The Gardens

When the direct Dillwyn Llewelyn line died out and Sir Charles had already left Penllergare to live in Newbridge-on-Wye they left a Victorian garden paradise of classic design stretching for several miles along the banks of the River Llan. There were great banks of azaleas and rhododendrons, trees from expeditions all over the world and

Robert Stafford, florist gardener c.1880/1900

rare exotic plants which can still be found today in some unspoilt areas along the river. These lived in a microclimate brought about by the steep slopes of the river banks and by the clever positioning of trees to protect the less hardy plants. In the spring when all the azaleas and rhododendrons came into flower the air was filled with their scent and their mass colour was magnificent. The more exotic species were close to the house protected by trees. Some of these won Awards of Merit with the RHS and one of them called *Pen'gare* is at Kew Gardens in London. Most were brought back after expeditions to the Far East and China.

There were kingfishers, woodpeckers with their brilliant feathers and all kinds of owls including the white owl. There was also a huge rookery with several hundred rooks that you could hear from miles away, even as far as the village on quiet summer nights. Our neighbour, George Williams, who lived in the thatched-roof cottage next door to us was a gamekeeper at Penllergare and he used to shoot and eat them as well as wood pigeons. There is even an oak tree several hundred years old and they used to call this owl's oak (coeden gwdihw). Some native oaks can live for over one thousand years. There were several brooks leading to the river that had engineered pools along their courses. These were filled with pungent watercress, which I sometimes used to collect and take home to my mother. The river was always full of brown trout, which were occasionally offered to my mother together with rabbits. My mother used to make sure that I ate watercress as a source of iron because I wouldn't eat cooked cabbage or greens. My mother also put Sanatogen and sometimes burgundy in my lemonade which were a natural form of iron supplement but little did I know it except that I had a tremendous appetite which is ridiculous because I was very thin. After the big sale of contents in 1936, the task of distributing the books in the Llewelyn library that did not go to Lysdinam fell to the parson Rev. D. P. Glyn Davies. Some were given to my father, i.e. *The Vine and Its Cultivation* and several books on Ancient Egypt and the Pyramids.

E. Vyron Williams, 2000

Exhibiting

Many of us who are connected with the National Auricula and Primula Society recollect how some years ago grand specimens of show varieties of the former used to be brought up from Penllergare to the exhibitions of South Kensington, where Sir John used to enter the list against our best gardeners, and even exhibit in the large class for fifty varieties. I need hardly say his frames contained the best varieties in commerce and in considerable numbers; while the species of Primula were grown in large quantities and always exhibited in fine condition, and Mr. Stafford the excellent gardener who superintended his florist flowers, used to be especially gratified when, after his long and toilsome journey, he was congratulated on the manner in which the exhibits were set up.

H. Honeywood D' Dombrain
The Gardener's Magazine, 21st September 1895

Alison's Story

All through my childhood, particularly at family gatherings, Penllergare was a name that frequently came up in conversation. It has been with me ever since I can remember and it was Penllergare that became the catalyst for my journey into the past.

At the parish church of Llangyfelach on 12th August 1838 John Williams and Mary Davies were married. He was a mason and she a mantuamaker. Both their fathers were colliers and, at the time, the Davies family lived at Middle Lodge. John and Mary set up home at Caerbadell and eventually had four children. Years later a painting of Mary Williams (née Davies) by Emma Charlotte Crichton, the daughter of John Dillwyn Llewelyn,

Portrait of Mary Williams by Emma Charlotte Crichton (née Dillwyn Llewelyn)

was given by her daughter, Mrs. Christie of Llangoed Castle, to Mary's daughter Margaret Bevan (née Williams). Margaret and her husband O. J. Bevan ran the Cross Stores in Penllergaer village. Tucked into the back of one of the paintings was the marriage certificate of John and Mary. Their son William married Hannah Rees whose family all lived at Weaver's Lodge (Middle Lodge).

William and Hannah Williams raised a family of eleven children, all of whom in various capacities were involved in work at Penllergare. My grandfather was their son Aneurin who sadly became an alcoholic and ended his days as a gravedigger, partly to fund his thirst. Despite this he was a man who had a passion for poetry. His great nephews remember him quoting Shakespeare as he dug the graves.

Penllergare is fantastic and magical. When I visited I could visualise that once glorious garden just by seeing the little rocky steps we walked down and all the ferns and trees. I had such a sense of nostalgia because I knew this was where my family came from. My great, great grandfather worked as a gardener so part of that place is my heritage. I could imagine my great, great grandmother in that tiny, two-up two-down cottage bringing up all those children. It took me back in time walking the paths they walked, looking at a tree and wondering if my great, great grandfather planted it. Seeing the church where William worked on the new extension and where his son Aneurin, my grandfather, helped build the surrounding wall brought it home to me how important Penllergare was to their very existence. Many of my family are in the graveyard at St. David's. Eventually the family spread out and moved away but they all came back to be buried at Penllergaer. Some were widowed, others married again and, crazy as it sounds, some were buried with their first wife or husband because they had already bought the plot!

Alison Pullen
2005

Uncle Aneurin

I loved Uncle Aneurin. He used to dig graves and was very well educated although he was self-taught. My brother and I used to sit on the tumps of earth and listen to him as he was digging and he would recite Shakespeare and other poetry to us. Mind you, we had to be careful, as the lower down he got, the more bones and old silver and metal coffin plates he threw up. It could be quite dangerous at times.

Jeffrey Phillips
in conversation, 2005

The Journey Back to Penllergare

My grandmother had kept an old marriage certificate in an ancient cardboard box, a cardboard box with 'Jaeger' on the label and a pencil scribble that read 'Men's Trunks – All Wool – Size 44 – Colour/Natural'. The certificate was a key piece of evidence that opened up a window on my ancestry and was to lead me, in the early 1990s, to the Llewelyn family home at Penllergare near Swansea.

The marriage certificate was of Daniel Rees aged thirty-seven years to Mary Davies aged twenty-six. Daniel was resident at Lower Lodge and Mary was the daughter of a farmer called James Davies who I think had been a farmer at Home Farm. The marriage took place in 1883 and Mary was Daniel's second wife, his first wife Elizabeth having died a few years earlier after the birth of twins. Mary also took on eleven of his children!

I realised then that Daniel was my great, great grandfather and that he had spent all his life at Penllergare. Since his first marriage he had lived at Lower Lodge, Cadle and it was from here that he was buried in St. David's Church in 1899. Before that he had grown up with his siblings at Weaver's Lodge (later called Middle Lodge). His father John Rees was a mason and had come with his wife Ann from a previous job at Middleton Hall, Carmarthenshire.

My grandmother, Violet Mary Evans (née Hill) was born in Gorseinon and was a granddaughter of Daniel Rees. She had been given to her aunt, Hannah Rees, who

Daniel Rees and his first wife Elizabeth who, after their marriage, set up home in Lower Lodge

had left Penllergare to run the post office in the High Street, Gilfach Goch. I was brought up in the 1970s listening to tales and anecdotes about Penllergare. How it was Daniel's job to empty the sewer; how Auntie Hannah remembered opening the gate at Lower Lodge for the visitors to travel up the drive and how we had the best rhubarb in Wales because it came from the gardens at Penllergare. Obviously a root of rhubarb had been brought up to Gilfach Goch at one time or another by one of my relatives on a visit. The rhubarb continues to thrive in my parents' garden today!

The Rees family was extensive in number and it seems that I have many connections with people who once worked on the estate. My great, great grandmother, Florence Hill (née Rees) had eleven brothers and sisters, nearly all of whom were born at Penllergare. Her sister Annie Mathias (née Rees) was a lady's maid at

Iris and Bronwen Rees, grandchildren of Daniel, whose parents emigrated to South Africa but kept the Welsh traditions

the Big House and travelled extensively with the Llewelyns. Florence had a cousin called George Williams who was Sir John Talbot Dillwyn Llewelyn's huntsman and gamekeeper and further relatives included Margaret Bevan of the Cross Stores, the Phillips family of Brynrhos Farm and the Venn family who later lived in Mumbles.

The Gardener's House

Daniel's son Charles Rees entered the ministry and became an Anglican priest. He ended his years as vicar of St. Margaret's Aberaman in Aberdare but came back to be buried by the wall in the graveyard of St. David's Church, Penllergaer with his wife Mary. Daniel's sister Hannah Rees married William Williams. They lived at Llwyn-yr-Eos cottage with their family and many of them worked at Penllergare during the latter part of the nineteenth century.

Finally, I found myself standing at the graves of John and Ann Rees and of Daniel and Elizabeth Rees in the churchyard of St. David's in Penllergaer. I felt a great sense of belonging at that moment. I realised that these people had dedicated their lives to the service of one family who, exceptionally for the time, had treated their employees well.

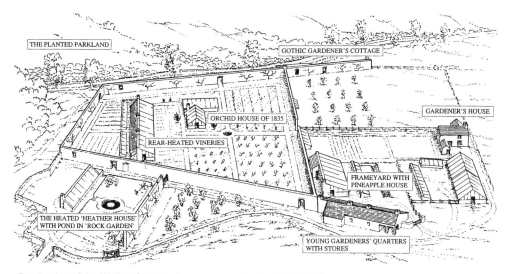

Realisation of the Walled Gardens from a survey by the RCAHMW

Labels within the image:
THE PLANTED PARKLAND
GOTHIC GARDENER'S COTTAGE
GARDENER'S HOUSE
ORCHID HOUSE OF 1835
REAR-HEATED VINERIES
FRAMEYARD WITH PINEAPPLE HOUSE
THE HEATED 'HEATHER HOUSE' WITH POND IN 'ROCK GARDEN'
YOUNG GARDENERS' QUARTERS WITH STORES

Although I had managed to find the church that day, not being from the locality, I still knew nothing of the estate and its whereabouts. Later with a map I roamed the grounds on my own in the rain. I could not believe my eyes when I discovered the remains of the lakes, the footpaths that sloped down the sides of the hills to the water features, the extensive varieties of trees and foliage and the remains of the constructed waterfalls. Were my ancestors here on hot August evenings? Were they building those steps with their masonry skills? Were my distant relatives preparing bonfires here in days past? Were they cutting grass and clearing leaves from pathways in autumn? Apparently so! A tremendous feeling of excitement and exhilaration went through me at that moment. A feeling of loneliness too, for I was a solitary figure in a vast landscape. But I felt as if I was a part of this land and a part of its history.

Dean Evans
2005

The Warmingtons

*[Charles Warmington became the Head Gardener after John Nunns
and stayed for fifty years.]*

Mary Eleanor Warmington known as Nelly was the daughter of Charles Warmington, the Head Gardener at Penllergare in the time of John Talbot D.L. She married William T. Rosser and they lived a couple of doors up from my mother in Swansea Road. Her mother, Jane Warmington, used to give painting lessons in the Gardener's House where they lived and my Auntie Annie used to go there for classes. My mother said that old Warmington was so mean he wouldn't give you an apple and the place was full of apples and quinces. There was a beautiful quince in the garden just outside their house. My mother would pass by on her way to play tennis and he used to sit at the window and watch, just to make sure no one picked anything.

Jeffrey Phillips
in conversation, 2005

The Kitchen Garden

The kitchen garden, which lies high and exposed to the north-east, contains five acres, the forcing and plant houses, melon ground, gardener's house, and bothy. The inner portion of the garden is enclosed by walls, and the outer portion by tall hedges and shrubberies for shelter. The ground is laid out in convenient quarters for cropping, which are divided by gravel walks. The borders on either side of the principal walks are planted with espalier and pyramidal fruit trees at suitable distances from the walk. The trees, however, do not grow freely nor bear fruit satisfactorily on account of the exposed situation of the garden. It is different with the trees on the walls, which grow vigorously and mature heavy crops of fruit in good seasons. There is a good peach wall here with a projecting framework of glass under the coping, which affords protection to a fine lot of trees in the best of health, and at the time of my visit were laden with fruit the size of pigeons' eggs. The varieties consisted of Lord Palmerston, one of the best of the large late varieties which ripen at the end of September; Prince of Wales, another excellent late variety, fruit tender, melting and juicy; Barrington, an old standard variety that should be grown in every collection; Early Alfred, which ripens in the beginning of August; Dr. Hogg, an excellent variety ripening in August; and Hardwick Nectarine, which is one of the hardiest and most prolific in cultivation. The different quarters in the kitchen garden were cropped systematically, each being filled with vegetables of one kind, the dwarfer and choicer sorts by themselves, and the cooler and stronger-growing kinds were treated in like manner, a quarter being devoted to rhubarb, artichokes, asparagus, peas, etc. The smaller fruits – gooseberries, currants, raspberries and straw-berries – were grown on the same principle.

The Melon Ground is one of the best I have seen for some time. It is convenient to the forcing and plant houses, and is completely shut in and sheltered by high hedges. It contains a good many pits and frames for bedding and other plants, and plenty of open space for growing and plunging plants during the summer and for storing hardy plants in winter. It is here that the seedling rhododendrons, azaleas and coniferous plants are grown in boxes until they are sufficiently large to be bedded out in nursery lines. Mr. Warmington had growing here an excellent assortment of *Liliums* in 11-inch pots . . . They were growing in a compost of equal parts of peat and loam, which seemed to suit them admirably.

Andrew Pettigrew
The Journal of Horticulture and Cottage Gardener
June/July 1886

The Edge Family

[From a letter written to Michael Norman.]

We ran a nurseryman business in the Walled Gardens which my family took over on 25th March 1928. I lived with my family in what was known as the Head Gardener's House. We rented the gardens after the death of Sir John Llewelyn Bart. and ran it for twelve years until we were given twelve months notice because the Bible College of Wales intended to buy the mansion and gardens when they had raised the necessary cash. Victor Williams worked for us for a couple of years when he was a young lad.

Their workmen and students knocked off all the plaster on the outside walls and cemented them all round. They did a lot of painting of the cornices etc. in the Library and elsewhere. The deal fell through when the cash was not raised.

Then the war came and the American Army took over the house and when they left, vandals took over and stole the lead etc. Finally, a few years later the Territorial Army blew up the mansion.

William Edge
24th July 1994

Private collection

Garden path, c.1850. Photograph by John Dillwyn Llewelyn

Iron Well, between the lakes, on the River Llan. Photograph by John Dillwyn Llewelyn

. . . Into the Woods

A Walk with Papa

A very busy day, I photographed and gardened, and after that had a walk with Papa, to the Lower Lake, where we found, in the upper part, where it is silting up considerably, how soon bogbeans grow in such localities. They grow luxuriantly in half-watery places which would not bear the weight of a man, and yet <u>looked</u> safe enough! We observed a number of May flies hovering over the water in the river, and just dipping in as they danced over it, – fragile creatures of a day, which was fast closing, – many of them probably destined to have their naturally short existence made even shorter, and thus to become of that use which everything in Nature possesses, by becoming food for the finny inhabitants of the stream.

Thereza Dillwyn Llewelyn
11th June 1856

The Natural World of Penllergare

Sadly the nineteenth century designed landscape of Penllergare has become damaged, neglected and overgrown but not all has vanished because a natural layer has formed over the top, protecting what lies hidden underneath. Time and Nature have transformed the place into a wildlife sanctuary, albeit with the remnants of its famous horticultural past still showing in places if you know where to look.

Penllergare with its distinct natural zones of steep wooded hillside, open grassland and damp water margins is a hugely varied habitat for a range of wild flowers, grasses, trees, fungi, insects and birdlife. On the north-western slope there are examples of

65

exotic species of trees dating back to the early nineteenth century, notably Japanese red cedar, sequoia, wellingtonia and monkey puzzle and these are under-planted with original specimens of rhododendron that, in early spring, bring colour contrast to the native and invasive *R. ponticum.* A mature swamp cypress sits on the valley floor not far from the yew grove planted by John Dillwyn Llewelyn on the ruins of an old mill. At the top of the hill is a fern-spray cypress possibly the rarest tree on the estate and maybe the biggest specimen in Britain. Native species of ash, beech (including several impressive copper beeches), lime, yew, birch and hemlock jostle for light with native and imported oaks. Several species of oak have been identified: – turkey, evergreen holm, red, sessile and common oak.

Wildflowers are abundant throughout the growing season from the early wood anemones, coltsfoot, golden saxifrage and wood sorrel of March and April closely followed by primroses and bluebells; to the later pyramid and marsh orchids and rosebay willowherb, foxglove, tormentil, red campion, ragged robin, meadowsweet and enchanter's nightshade that appear in midsummer, as well as the invasive Himalayan balsam. These are only a few of the hundreds of species to be seen during the summer months. An unwelcome invader is the bracken that covers much of the grassland, suppresses less robust species and is also subject to arson, which causes additional damage. Some rare plants have been discovered, that possibly escaped from the mansion's formal gardens. Clumps of solomon's seal, royal and buckler fern, Himalayan honeysuckle, three varieties of bamboo and a distinctive pendula sedge have migrated into the park. A giant knotweed (non-invasive) called *Fallopia sachalinensis* has been discovered near the Afon Llan and bog asphodel and whorled caraway, (two species included by CCW in Category A of their List of Globally Threatened Plants) have recently been found during an ecological survey.

Cleaner now, after suffering years of industrial pollution, the Afon Llan once more supports aquatic life. The heron is often found at the edge of the Fishpond (Upper Lake) through where the river flows and ducks and moorhens also breed. River fish are increasing and the water margins are also important breeding grounds for toads and frogs. Because of its wooded seclusion many species of birds nest and/or feed at Penllergare. Over fifty species of birds were identified in recent surveys. The tawny owl is known to nest here. The most observed birds are the wren, robin, wood pigeon, blackbird and chaffinch. There have been sightings of buzzard, red kite, great spotted woodpecker, sparrow-hawk, dipper, song thrush and yellow wagtail; and in recent years there have been several reports of a kingfisher by the waterfall!

Mammals are less apparent on the estate due to their shy or nocturnal habits. Rabbits abound on the southern grassy slopes, evidence of the fox has been seen and the northern wooded area is an ideal habitat for the ubiquitous grey squirrel. Badgers are known to live on the site and ecologists tell us this is ideal territory for the otter. During the nineteenth century otters were hunted for sport at Penllergare and together with later pollution their numbers have greatly diminished. However, the mink has moved in and can be seen occasionally by the river bank. At dusk bats are to be seen flitting among the trees.

Where there is a proliferation of flowering plants butterflies are familiar visitors. Look out for the butterfly bush (*Buddleja davidii*) which is a favourite feeding ground. Penllergare plays host among many others to the red admiral, tortoiseshell, peacock, brimstone, large white, the ringlet, clouded yellow, orange tip, meadow brown and common blue, plus many moths, damsel, hover and dragonflies.

Whatever the season the ecological riches of Penllergare are there for everyone to see. Even the most inexperienced of botanists and ornithologists will find much to discover armed with no more than a small identifying book and a sharp eye. People are encouraged to enjoy the peaceful seclusion of Penllergare Valley Woods and experience not only the beauty of the place but also its diversity of wildlife.

Jennie Eyers, 2003
Based on information supplied by Pryce Consultant Ecologists (2002),
The Shared Earth Trust (2001) and Keith Clements (2000)

The Longest Day

As about 12 o'clock it set in wet and continued so . . . Being a fine morning we all set off for the lower lake to witness an otter hunt; we only saw the commencement, and after that were driven to take shelter in the boathouse, whence we could <u>hear</u> but not see much of the hunt. To amuse ourselves till dinner came, some occupied themselves in lighting a fire and collecting sticks and dead leaves sufficiently dry and light etc. – after a deal of trouble and consequently amusement, the fire was made to burn beautifully, and when bacon and eggs arrived they were fried by Mama and Emma, and highly approved of when in an edible condition! After lunch we returned home . . . I saw Papa make two sterioscopes, with the new sterioscopic camera that he gave me for my birthday present. I intend to work hard with it, so as to get some pictures worthy of it; for, as Papa says, there are first rate subjects here to be done.

Thereza Dillwyn Llewelyn
19th June 1856

Private collection

Watercolour of Lower Lake, looking north, showing the Boathouse. Artist unknown but probably a member of the Dillwyn Llewelyn family

The Waterfall, Penllergare, c.1850.
Photograph by John Dillwyn Llewelyn

Magical Land of Secret Spaces

As a child in the 1960s I used to play among the ruins of Sir John Llewelyn's estate. In my blue anorak I would explore the magical land of secret spaces formed by the overgrown gardens. There were magnificent and exotic evergreens with interestingly textured trunks and in the months of May and June the greens would be ablaze with the gaudy oranges, pinks and reds of the rhododendrons. With other children I used to swim in the river below the waterfall and remember the Monkey Puzzle trees. As a very young child I would be taken around the tumbledown lodges by my father in my pushchair. We would repeat a mantra – in Welsh – about the poor, sad little houses with no roof, no windows and no one to live there. My Father was a builder, so he must have been quite upset by the sad demise of these little lodges.

Helen Phillips
2004

Days Out

My parents, Bessie and Aneurin John, loved the countryside. In the 1930s we lived just outside Llangyfelach which, at that time, was surrounded by fields. Everyone walked in those days before the war and they took us children regularly for days out at Penllergare. We walked there in spring to see the rhododendrons and azaleas and to smell the heady scent that seemed to hang over the valley like a cloud. Mother always said there was a better collection there than at Clyne. In summer we went for picnics, always with a large homemade sponge cake, then later on in the year for blackberrying and to gather mushrooms. When she was older my sister Buddug cycled there to meet her friends. I never learnt to keep my balance so never had a bike. Years later when I married, Peter and I would drive there and take our young son. Nigel, in his pushchair, clocked up many miles around Penllergare! When he was older Peter taught him to fish in the River Llan and the pair of them would spend days over there.

I remember the time my cousin Iwan and his friends got lost in the woods and had not returned by dark. My father and uncle went out to search for them and when Iwan got home, my aunt was so relieved she gave him a good hiding with the bamboo cane on the end of the feather duster. It didn't do him any harm.

Merlys Williams
2005

Valley Woods

When I go to the woods I hear
Chirping robins singing sweetly in the warm spring breeze,
Hooting owls in the dark black night,
Brown leaves crunching as I step on them.

When I go to the woods I see
Smooth stems swaying coldly in the breeze,
Trees causing problems for puzzled monkeys
The waterfall cascading into the lake.

When I go to the woods,
I touch the bark from the oak tree as hard as a brick,
I touch the metal wheel from a horse and cart of many years ago.
I touch the glittering spiky grass.

Liam Clayfield
Penllergaer Primary School, 2006

Memories of Freedom

At the age of eight in the early 1960s I remember leaving my prefab home and the lunar landscape of Pentrechwyth to arrive at a new house in Blaen-y-Maes and the open playground of the Penllergare Estate. My newly-made friends and I soon began exploring the area, meeting at Cadle Mill where we'd buy sweets at the little shop before setting off past the Big House gates and the old colliery workings to make our way up the Llan river. On this pretty little stretch of water we would spend hours paddling, swimming and exploring. I was one of those who jumped off the waterfall rocks into the plunge pool below and balanced along the fallen trees that stretched dangerously, yet invitingly, across the many meanders.

Derek Berry

The Waterfall

69

At the age of twelve I joined the Army Cadets' Fforestfach Detachment led by ex-army instructors. During weekends and holiday periods in the warmer months we would carry a huge twenty-man marquee between us up the old driveway and erect this on what must have been the mansion garden, for I remember the remains of the foundations and the walled garden being quite clearly visible. From this homely base we would set off early for the day, sometimes calling in at the A48 transport café (if we had money in our pocket), for a bacon sandwich breakfast with a mug of hot tea. Then the work would begin . . . making rope bridges across the Llan, constructing bivouacs (which we never slept in!) from fallen branches and ferns, playing orienteering games and learning all sorts of other 'bush craft' techniques. If the rain came, which it frequently did, we were given permission to collect a key and sleep in the Forestry Commission hut.

All of this is a long time ago now, but they are still happy memories of freedom in what to me was a wilderness waiting to be explored!

Brian Birt
2006

A Visit to the Woods in 2004

What I liked about Penllergare Valley Woods was all the trees that came from different countries. I saw trees from Chile, Australia and North America. There was a Monkey Puzzle tree that I like very much too. There was also another plant that I really liked. If you touch the plant it explodes [*Himalayan balsam*] and all the seeds come out and the wind blows them away to make new plants . . . The Waterfall was beautiful, even though it was a bit vandalised. We came across an unusual tree because if it gets caught in a fire then it won't die [*Sequoia*]. I saw lots of acorns that I liked, but I was a bit disappointed that I didn't see any conkers. There was a tree called a Japanese red cedar. I found some of its red bark on the ground and I took it home and gave it to my Mum.

Chris Cray

A path in the woods

If I had the money to change anything about the estate then I would change it into a proper country park, so that people would be able to go there and enjoy the scenery. I would like to get rid of the graffiti and clear up the rubbish from the pond so everything looks nicer. I even saw a supermarket trolley near the Waterfall. I think it would be a good idea to clear all the pond weed so the lake would look nice again, and you could see the water. I think that special barriers and ramps should be put up so people cannot joyride and burn their cars there. There should also be fences so people cannot get in and cause vandalism. It would be nice too if some of the old buildings were restored like the Observatory. But I do like visiting Penllergare Valley Woods.

Tyler Batt
Penllergaer Primary School, 2004

Exploring the Woods

Mention the name 'Penllergare' and I am taken back to the time when we were allocated a new council house in Portmead, Swansea in 1956. My late husband, Trevor, had been born and brought up in Llangyfelach so he knew the story of the Penllergare Estate and the Llewelyn family who had lived there. Cadle Mill was within a stone's throw of our new home and even though our youngest child was not yet walking, we would trundle him in his pushchair (the other two children trailing behind) and make our way 'into the woods' – passing the old disused coal mine at Tirdonkin where we looked for fossils.

Penetrating into the estate, we would make our way along a path to the old mansion – still standing, though in a more than dilapidated condition. The stone pillars of the portico gave an idea of the past grandeur of the house and I remember the atrium in the reception hall, still with the remains of stained glass. What a beautiful work that must have been in the 'days when', and how impressive that hall must have been to visitors. Amongst the rubble and fallen masonry, I recall seeing what remained of a statue or bust that must have adorned that part of the building. We did not venture into the remainder of the house, as we considered it too dangerous to look further. The vestiges of the formal garden remained, with unpruned rose bushes still maintaining some flowers, and there were the remains of a terrace.

There were many occasions when, asked by our neighbours' children if we were going 'over the woods', a number of them would accompany us, and we enjoyed showing them the various birds and other wildlife abundant in the area. We would identify wild flowers and Trevor would show the children how to make baskets out of the reeds growing by the river. Reaching the lake there would be time to indulge

Private collection

The Evans family fishing off the dam at Lower Lake, c.1960

The Evans children and friends on the mansion ruins, early 1960s

in 'fishing' with a pin on the end of a piece of string, and of course there were jam-jars for tadpoles to be collected in the still pools. The pool under the Waterfall was deep enough for Trevor to teach our children to swim. At times, we would halt in our tracks, pretending there might be Red Indians, and perhaps even wild bears and wolves in the dense forest. I think the children might even have believed this to be true! Taking a 'picnic', consisting usually of bread-and-jam and a bottle of 'pop', would enhance our day out.

It is great news that Penllergare is once again envisaged as a place that can be enjoyed by a new generation, and if they have only half the fun that we had fifty years ago, the restoration will be more than justified.

Eve Evans
2005

Of Steps and Stones and Monkey Tails

[Impressions by Year 5/6 Penllergaer Primary School, 2005]

When we started walking there were loads of different plants and creatures. We walked up a massive hill. There were about 100 steps and we had to count them on the way up. It was difficult because everyone kept on losing count. We were exhausted after that.

Cameron Kennedy

As soon as we entered the woods I saw how beautiful it was and it cheered me up. There was lots of plantlife and wildlife such as the Monkey Puzzle tree. The branches looked like lots of monkey tails. We found out which way the Mansion was facing because of the Monkey Puzzle in the photo.

Michael Payne

Penllergaer Primary School (Year 5/6) visit Valley Woods, 2005

At Penllergare Woods there is a lot to see. Firstly there is a man-made waterfall which is breathtakingly beautiful. There is also a quarry and an old observatory from which one of the first photographs of the moon was taken. There is also a lot to do in the woods such as taking walks, running along the side of the river, lounging on your back by the Waterfall and exploring the wildness of the undergrowth.

Caitlin Copp

Penllergaer Primary School (Year 5/6) 2005

We walked down the one and a half mile long drive that you can see where JDL's workers got dangerous gunpowder and blasted out the rock which they then used at the Waterfall. There was a spectacular view when we looked at the opposite side of the valley because you could see most of John Dillwyn Llewelyn's massive garden.

Robert Snell

We went to the woods to learn about Penllergare and its history. John Dillwyn Llewelyn used to live there in his mansion. It was demolished and is now the site of the council building. I felt calm and relaxed when I saw the water from the Waterfall crash down over the rocks into the river. We were right up close to it, and you could feel the droplets of water. It was lovely.

Joe Parker

Early Days in the Woods

It took us a while to find the Waterfall. We called it the 'Hidden Waterfall'. By this time I had a gang of friends and we went in search of this sound we could hear. We slid down the bank and hoped a tree would stop our fall. The rhododendrons were so thick it was like a jungle. There were no paths. We crawled our way through just following the sound until eventually we came out on top of the Waterfall. All the young people of my age knew every single thing that lived up here in the woods. We knew every nest, every shrew and water vole. We knew where they were on the river and there were masses of them. Nothing passed us by. There were otters here until the pollution wiped them out, that's when the mink took over. We named Tirdonkin Colliery 'Frog Mine' because there were hundreds of them in every puddle and under every stone. We loved Tirdonkin. We learned to rock climb up there. We used the buildings which were huge. The place had closed down and the entrances had been bricked up but we knocked some of the bricks out and crawled in. It was possible to climb down the shaft and get across from Gladys pit into Charles pit. They were side by side and had been named after two of the Dillwyn Llewelyn children. If I knew my kids were doing that I'd strangle them!

Last year when I was helping with the clearance in Valley Woods I came across this sycamore tree not far from the Waterfall. I cut all the ivy from it and suddenly realised

Michael Norman, Chris Meredith, Dai Whitelock and Simon Page comparing the line of a path with a JDL photograph, 2005

this was the tree my gang and I had carved our initials on in 1961 – and they were still there, quite faint, but still there. I must have been about nine at the time. I had just bought my first proper sheath knife and a short time after we had carved our initials I swapped it for a homing pigeon. This chap said keep it in for two weeks and then let it go and it will return home to you. Well, I did all that and let it go and it went straight back to his shed. I lost both the pigeon and my best knife. It was a lesson I never forgot. Nobody has conned me like that since.

All the children learnt to swim in Lower Lake. There was so much silt coming down the river that it made a sort of beach on every bend. You would find lots of local families down there, every ten feet or so, all on their own private beach. They had a fire going and a kettle boiling away on the top and they were there for the day, until it got dark. People came from Cadle, Portmead, Penlan as well as Blaen-y-Maes. It was our place – our park. The dads would dam the river in places to provide a pool for the younger children to learn to swim before they were allowed to go into the Lake. There were five weirs on the river and the middle one was the deepest and was known as 'the Kiddies'. You had to be able to swim to the island otherwise you stayed in the weir. You were really grown up when you could swim to the island.

David Whitelock
in conversation, 2006

Trees, Slides and Swings

Tree climbing became a favourite pastime with the children in the 1970s. Erin would chose a tree with many branches, climb to the top and then proceed to swing backwards and forwards until the tree was swaying like a pendulum. Deborah would select her favourite beech and disappear into the foliage. Then from the top of the tree a disembodied voice could be heard saying "I can see so much . . . I can see the motorway . . . I can see the mountains . . . Ooooh, I can see the sea" which was just great for her, because she could not be seen at all!

Another popular activity was to take a strong rope and an old line pulley and construct swings and aerial slides from the many suitable trees in Valley Woods. The girls then wished to share the excitement of the swings with friends. The height on the outward swing from the ground could be as much as forty feet and one of the first friends

Erin on her aerial pulley

to try promptly fell off but fortunately was not hurt. The next group of friends tried the swings once and were so frightened they were never seen again! Erin found a piece of electrical flex near the river that was only double core, and decided that she would make her own swing. She was warned that the flex would not support her weight but stubbornly went on to tie it to a tree and swing. I looked away and there was a thump. She had disappeared. Predictably the flex had snapped and she had fallen flat on her back on the riverbank, which had winded her so much she could speak only in a very high-pitched voice. That was her last venture into swing making. The pulley was used to create aerial slides across the river. The only problem was that the rope would sometimes work loose and one or other of the children would be deposited in the water, resulting in a quick return home.

Keith Clements
2005

From Portmead to Penllergare

In the 1960s we did not have a car, so on sunny weekends – and I seem to remember they were always sunny – we went for a walk in the woods. My father was familiar with Penllergare as he was brought up in Mynydd Bach and used to go there as a teenager.

It became such a novelty, our neighbouring friends wanted to come too. We packed a picnic and took plastic water flasks, wellies, fishing rods and nets. We did not use the main entrance, as we were frightened someone would stop us and 'tell the police' We were aware it was private property, but did not know exactly who owned it. We clambered down the steep embankment from the bridge in Cadle. Once we were beside the river we knew no-one could see us and were safe! The path was well defined, but muddy in places – hence the wellies.

When it was particularly hot we used to stop by the Lower Dam to dip our feet in the water but did not stay in there too long in case a lamprey attached itself to our legs! I remember the water being rust-coloured in places, which presumably was due to pollution. We used to watch the eels jump the weir and attempt to catch them. (One fisherman friend of the family often brought us some back to eat). I always marvelled at the rhododendrons and being a girl was fascinated by the array of colours, though I knew there were even prettier ones beyond the lake. They are still one of my favourite flowers today.

We passed dense clumps of bamboo and sometimes used them to shelter from the rain. The marsh marigolds were also special – but as they were in the bog it was impossible to reach them – and in any case they were off the beaten track and my father warned me not to go there. We continued up the riverbank until we reached the lake. Once the council 'bombed' open the bank to allow the lake to drain. We had to chance our luck crossing over the 'rapids' in the river, which were particularly unnerving following the heavy rains.

Jane and her brother in the pool below the Waterfall, early 1960s

Jennie Eyers

A 'beach' on the River Llan

When we arrived at the Lake we ventured to the left side (north – I think) that meant descending to the shore. It was almost sandy and closely resembled the beach. We chose that area as it was particularly sheltered from the wind and we were able to light small fires to dry ourselves after a swim. My brothers and I learnt to swim in the Lake – even though the water was freezing at times! While we waited for our mother to prepare the picnic, we skimmed stones across the water – the surface was always like glass and I remember my father always had the most 'skims'.

Following lunch, we continued up the lane. We now joined the main drive. This was more open and sunnier than the wooded path. Sometimes the banks of bracken on the hillside would be scorched black from the 'naughty boys' who had lit fires that had gone out of control. We continued up the driveway. To the right were even larger clumps of bamboo – but we rarely went down there as it was, generally, too far to walk. We passed one lodge, which I think was inhabited and then, another. The second one was derelict and only brick walls remained. From there a path led to a farmhouse at the top of the hill. My parents often speculated how wonderful it would be to live there. Once or twice we sneaked a look, but I think it was abandoned as I remember peering through windows and seeing plaster peeling off walls.

We continued up the Drive – with the right-hand side falling away into a very steep decline. As children, we were warned to stay away from the edge. There were brambles on the left-hand side, which precluded us from having a look up the hill (I now suspect that is where the Walled Garden is?). We stopped at the 'cave' for a rest. It was always cold, damp and mysterious and I often wondered what on earth it had been used for. It provided excellent shelter from heavy rain, but as we were now a long way from home we only stayed there a short while. There was often evidence of bonfires and bottles of beer where, presumably the 'naughty boys' had their parties!

To the right, we could hear the sound of rushing water and one day made a valiant effort to cut and force our way through the thick undergrowth of rhododendrons. When we reached the Waterfall we could hardly believe our eyes. It was magical. My brothers and I took a plunge into the deep pool – which was really freezing cold. I can remember thinking just how cold it was. We stayed there awhile, and returned many times after, but we made sure we lit a fire before we encountered the pool!

Our final onslaught was, in the early days, the mansion itself. I can remember the outline of a grand building, which was later surrounded with chain link fencing, with signs warning us not to go near. I vaguely remember standing on the steps and my mother has photographs to prove it. The monkey tree was there and as predicted, there were the most beautiful of rhododendrons and azaleas, both on the right and left-hand side, down the steep ravine. We were allowed another 'play' and drink here before we set off home. We dared to go home following the Drive all the way to the bottom. We thought the 'men' would have gone home by now! This route was not as spectacular as the river path, but we were privy to the wonderful scent and different varieties of azaleas as we neared the end of the Drive.

Pen y Fro Primary School (Year 5) admiring the Japanese red cedar

As one of the socio-economically poor of Portmead . . . Penllergare was, and is, one of my most favourite haunts. It cost nothing but exercise. When I was an adult, I was always wary of going there alone as in the 80s there were tales of drug addicts and reprobates scouring the woods. The innocence of the 60s was lost but the magic remained.

Jane Hanley
2005

Woodland Views

[Year 6. Llangyfelach Primary School, 2005]

I loved seeing the Waterfall. I also really liked the views from the bridge which were tremendous. I really couldn't believe Penllergare was a home to so many animals and I don't want to see that being taken away from them, because it is such a lovely place.

Naomi Machin

It was brilliant when they told us about all the different trees. My favourites were the Monkey Puzzle and the red cedar. Thank you too for telling us about evergreen and deciduous trees.

Rebecca Jones

Most of all I liked the Waterfall. I did not know anything about John Dillwyn Llewelyn or his family until our walk around Penllergare Valley Woods.

Harry Isaac

Keith Clements demonstrating a plateway to schoolchildren, 2005

It was really interesting being in the forest. It was funny when we all counted the steps and had different answers. The Waterfall was wonderful and it was hand made. My favourite tree was the Monkey Puzzle because of its branches.

Lauren Lewis

I would like to improve Penllergare Woods by clearing the plants from the lake, so that the lake would be visible and beautiful.

Christopher Griffiths

Jennifer Cloke

Picnic in the woods with Pontlliw and Llangyfelach Primary Schools, 2006

Natural Resources

In the 1970s identifying flowers, trees and birds was an important part of our enjoyment of the woods and bird watching at Penllergare became a favourite activity. We each of us had our own binoculars. It was a bizarre sight to see a very young and small Erin walking along the tracks with the strap of the binoculars so long that they were banging into her kneecaps. Nevertheless, sore knees apart, we managed to identify many of the species that are still present today.

The owl population was larger then and provided an abundance of pellets that were collected and soaked in water to remove the fur and feathers. The bones and teeth that remained were assembled into proper order as skeletons and mounted on black card and taken to school to show others. Sadly, both teachers and pupils could not understand what had been done and showed no interest in the skill required to present the reassembled bones!

We regularly collected mushrooms that were then cooked and eaten. When I informed them that other fungi were also edible, it was decided to give it a try. One of the first

Jennie Eyers

experiments was a bracket fungus that grows on birch. I think the girls chose it because of its size. It was duly taken home, carefully prepared and fried. We sat down and with much anticipation started to munch our way through this woodland delicacy. For some moments there was not a sound and then Deborah announced "My wellies would have tasted better than this". From then on we stuck to field mushrooms!

Keith Clements
2005

Pontlliw schoolchildren near the Waterfall, 2005

78

Penllergare Valley Woods

When I go to Penllergare Woods
I hear birds twittering around the wood,
Water gushing down the waterfall,
Owls all night around the woods hooting.
When I go to Penllergare Woods,
I like to touch the rough bark on the trees,
The soft moss and the grass all around.

Cara Nunn
Penllergaer Primary School, 2006

Wildlife

The girls were always interested in all the wildlife in the woods but reptiles were an unfailing fascination as they are so secretive and rarely seen. Occasionally a grass snake or an adder would be glanced as they disappeared into the vegetation. The same would occur with lizards, which were even more difficult to observe. All reptiles love warmth so we selected a large piece of wood, placed it in a sunny spot and left it for several days. Later, when we lifted the board adders, grass snakes and slow worms would be squirming off in all directions. Both children knew how to handle these creatures and did so with confidence. Not so their friends, who would run screeching in all directions when shown a harmless grass snake. Sunning stones were placed for lizards and we were very lucky we were able to observe these rare and elusive animals at close quarters.

The children have now grown up and left home but I have continued my association with Penllergare and it never ceases to fascinate. Twenty-five years later it is a pleasant surprise to find almost the same number of flower species and birds existing there. Valley Woods still holds many hidden surprises even though archaeological surveys are uncovering much evidence of the past. Penllergare has been described as 'a secret and magical place', it is slowly revealing its secrets but, to me, it will never lose its magic.

Eric Hughes

Keith Clements
2005

Upper Lake in autumn

79

Jennifer Cloke

The Observatory

Observations

Star Gazing

. . . being dark, we went to the dear old Observatory and lionised Mlle, Emma and John as far as Jupiter, Venus, Pleiades etc. I love the telescope dearly. A splendid night for definition. Arietis was very clear and sharp, and Jupiter's belts very marked and black.

Thereza Dillwyn Llewelyn
25th December 1856

Snow fell with rain in the morning, the greatest contrast from yesterday. It cleared up beautifully in the afternoon and so went for a walk. I got D. Mandre to refasten the Thermometer which had got loosened by the storm, and to alter the Telescope-camera; and when it was done I showed him and his son, 'Venus'. They were very much pleased, and wonder stricken, and David exclaimed "It is as big as the Moon!" It is not the first time I have heard that comparison made! The reason, most likely is, that the moon is the only large heavenly body that they can compare with the magnified object.

Thereza Dillwyn Llewelyn
20th January 1857

I looked through Uncle John's big telescope and saw the moon which looked like Gruyere cheese and also saw Jupiter and three of his moons; the fourth was eclipsed by himself. Harry [*her brother*] and I returned to Hendrefoilan by moonlight.

Amy Dillwyn
1864

I remember at quite an early age (possibly the late 1920s) my father taking my brother and me into the Observatory and setting us up so that we could take it in turns to look through the telescope. What an amazing land of stars! I remember being introduced to an array of twinkling lights. It was always a wonderful occasion to be taken inside. He and my mother introduced us to the Plough and how to recognise its shape and from that we found the Pole Star and, from that, Cassiopeia – lovely sounding names.

Betty Richards
2005

The Observatory looked nice though it did have cracks and shots from the soldiers who were there in World War II and who used it for target practice.

Zak Evans
Llangyfelach Primary School, 2005

The Observatory Garden 1886

The Observatory garden, which is entirely devoted to the culture of the rarest and choicest florist flowers, is laid out in small oblong beds for minutely observing the plants and flowers at all stages of their growth. Besides these and rockeries, it contains a great many pits and frames for growing rare and tender varieties. The large collections of auricula, carnation, primula, pansy and other florist flowers grown here can scarcely be surpassed, if indeed equalled, in any private place in the kingdom. What is called the new garden adjoins this, and is partly enclosed by large shrubberies. It is a delightful piece of undulating pleasure ground tastefully laid out and planted with the choicest kinds of trees and shrubs. Amongst coniferous trees were good specimens of *Cryptomeria japonica, Thuiopsis borealis, Cupressus Lawsoniana, Wellingtonia gigantea, Araucaria imbricata*, hemlock spruce and many others, ranging in height from thirty to sixty feet and furnished to the ground with the most luxuriant growth. The bank of rhododendrons and azaleas were magnificent, and arranged in colour so as to produce the best effect while in flower. The broad gravel walks which wind through it are bordered by rich shrubberies, rare flowering plants and well kept short grass. The garden contains a good lawn tennis ground for recreation, and a cosy summer house to rest in and shun the heat, or to shelter from pelting showers. In an adjacent shady pine plantation Mr. Llewelyn showed us a collection of some of the new and more tender kinds of rhododendrons that he is trying to inure to the climate of Penllergare. The plants were making strong, healthy growths, and Mr. Llewelyn is sanguine that many of them will prove hardy when planted in sheltered situations in the woods.

Andrew Pettigrew
The Journal of Horticulture and Cottage Gardener
June /July 1886

Jennie Eyers

Betty Richards talking to Llangyfelach Primary School children at the Observatory, 2005

The Observatory Garden 1927-1936

Our sitting room looked out onto the Observatory garden. There was a formal garden nearest to the house and the large window had a window-sill low enough for me to climb over and get outside quickly. The grassy path and bank made it easy to get into the main garden itself. The Conservatory on the left as you came out of the house had its entrance on the drive side of the iron railings and a gravel path led across the lawn over to the Observatory on both sides of a very large oak tree, with nearby a small watercourse leading down to a rockery. The beds contained beautiful groups of azaleas and the shrubbery, on the edge of the drive, had a variety of colourful trees and plants right up to the side of the Observatory. On the right there was a long stone wall which bordered the back drive and ran along the top edge of the laundry drying ground which was on the lower level. The wall continued all along the back drive up to the Observatory where a wooden door in the wall could lead into the Observatory from the drive. This was always kept locked. Inside the wall were fan-trained peach trees and pear trees and a row of quite large frames for propagation. To hide these from the garden was a beech hedge which always looked trim and neat. It was a lovely enclosed garden, good for picnics!

On top of the bank outside the window were two date palm trees, one quite tall and the other less than half its height. I loved the furry trunks and learned that the pieces sticking out were the discarded leaf fronds. The flowers on the top always looked very feathery and were a yellowy colour. In the spring the garden was very colourful with many forms of narcissus and daffodils as well as many different azaleas. It was the more common yellow azalea that seemed to have the sweetest scent, but all the colours blended in so well. As well as the oak tree there were two very large fir trees, one with hanging curved branches.

Betty Richards
2005

Private collection

The Observatory, c.1852/3 – photograph by John Dillwyn Llewelyn

A Unique Building

The remains of the Observatory stand in the grounds. This Observatory is one of the most unique buildings in Wales . . . it consists of an entrance, a large room for developing and a room where the telescope stood. It was originally built by John Dillwyn Llewelyn for his daughter Thereza in the 1850s. One of the first pictures of the moon was taken from here and a copy of the original glass photo plate is in the National Museum of Wales in Cardiff.

Jennie Bowen, aged 11, 1977
Penllergaer Primary School project

Looking down into the laboratory

Equatorial Observatory

The Observatory consists of a circular dressed masonry telescope chamber 5.5 metres in diameter; the lower part has walls 80 cm thick, but the upper part, to a height of 4 metres, has walls reduced to about 30 cm. The inside of the Observatory is lined with hollow clay bricks which are interspersed with wooden blocks set in a regular pattern and on which were fixed 4" x ½" tongued and grooved wall cladding set on battens. These bricks not only acted in preventing vibrations from entering the building but they also retained thermal heat in the Observatory. Within the observing chamber is a 3 metre deep annular pit which was floored over with timber. Occupying the centre of this circular pit is a conical pillar, the top part of which is mainly comprised of bricks on which rested and revolved a top shaped stone with three small iron levelling plates which supported the telescope. The mounting resembled a small naval gun and it had wheels to control the elevation and rotary motion. The object of the pillar and pit was to protect the telescope from seismic-type external vibrations. Its unusual shape suggests that photographic experiments were an important consideration in its design.

The Observatory was designed with a large wooden dome or cupola, in the shape of a top hat, clad in

The pulley system and shutter

The telescope pedestal

83

copper sheeting with white leaded paint to minimise the rise of convector currents which would affect the clarity of vision from the telescope. The top of the semi-circular dome projected slightly above the movable cylindrical top member and was made to revolve upon a geared ring mounting which rotated on roller bearings fixed to the top of the masonry structure. This movement has been calculated as one degree in four minutes. This brought the observation aperture into line with whatever part of the heavens the telescope was directed at and gave between ten to fifteen degrees angle of view. The wheel controlling this movement, was fixed vertically on the floor with the lower part recessed into the floor. There was a side shutter consisting of two 'doors' and a roof shutter that exposed half the diameter.

On the east side and attached to the Observatory, is a building, approximately 3 metres in width x 6 metres in length, which was possibly a laboratory and darkroom associated with the astronomical use of photography . . . This room has a fireplace, evidence of a wooden floor, and a flight of wooden steps leading to the telescope mounting.

It is likely that the first astronomical photographs in Wales were taken at the Observatory as it is known lunar photographs were taken from the building c.1855. One of the earliest photographs taken of the moon was the work of John D. Llewelyn with the help of his daughter Thereza. Notes written by Thereza some time later state: "about 1855 he made a photo of the moon, and as moonlight requires much longer exposure it was my business to keep the telescope moving steadily as there was no clockwork action".

Malcolm Hill, C.Eng. FICE
An extract from *Penllergaer and the Llewelyns*

Scent and Colour

Springtime in Penllergare was wonderful. In the early 1960s my husband Graham helped run the St. David's scout troop with the late Denzil Mossford and they used to have a twenty-four hour camp for the younger scouts in the grounds not far from the mansion. I often went along too. On one occasion I climbed up some wooden steps into the half-ruined Observatory onto a sort of circular platform. There was no roof and I was able to look out over this sea of rhododendrons. The colours were amazing. I had never seen such blooms before in my life and the scent from the azaleas was intoxicating. There is a yellow one like it now at Clyne and just smelling it brings back memories of Penllergare all those years ago.

Beryl Quirk
2005

Sir John Talbot Dillwyn Llewelyn (1836–1927)

Sir J. T. D. Llewelyn, the second child of John Dillwyn Llewelyn was born on 25th May 1836 at Penllergare. He was educated at Eton and Christchurch, Oxford, where he graduated with an MA in 1859. In the summer of 1855, during his vacations from Oxford, he was the leader of a party that excavated a bronze age barrow at Mynydd Garngoch, a piece of wasteland on the Penllergare estate. At the time he became President of the Cambrian Archaeological Association and was a member for seventy-one years. When he was at Oxford, being a keen cricketer, he frequently brought down parties to play against local teams. He was stated to be a very good bowler but a poor batsman and is reputed to have once bowled out the famous W. G. Grace in his younger days. *[He became the first Chairman of Glamorgan County Cricket Club when it was founded in 1888, and President of the Welsh Rugby Union between 1885-1906. His keen interests in horticulture were demonstrated by his being a Vice-President of the Royal Horticultural Society.]*

On 7th May 1861 John married Caroline Julia, eldest daughter of Sir Michael Hicks Beach, 8th Baronet, M.P. and sister of the famous Chancellor of Exchequer, Lord St. Aldwyn. The couple had four sons, John Michael, William, Charles and Henry, together with three daughters, Gwendoline Harriet, Mary Caroline and Gladys Mary. Three of the children died in childhood.

Sir John was much involved in the public life of the Swansea area, more so than his father J. D. Llewelyn whose main interests were for his scientific pursuits. Sir John was a Justice of the Peace, a Deputy Lieutenant of the County, High Sheriff for Glamorganshire in 1878 and Mayor of Swansea in 1891. He was created a Baronet by Queen Victoria in the New Year Honours List of 1890.

His contest for the parliamentary seat in 1895 was well reported in the local newspaper and on 18th July its headlines read: 'Triumphant majority for Sir John Llewelyn . . . Swansea has broken her record of sixty years and returned a Unionist Member to the House of Commons'. He held the seat until 1900. Possessed of a vigorous grasp of the political and social problems of his day Sir John stood high in the esteem of the people as a very broad-minded man and an ideal landlord. In religion he was a Protestant and Churchman, in politics he was a Conservative.

Long before the Education Act of 1870 he and his family had maintained elementary schools for boys and girls, and they did not cease their interest in the new schools when the responsibility for teaching passed into other hands. Sir John acted as one of the Managers of the School Group for Swansea who were appointed by the Glamorgan County Council. He was also a governor of the Gowerton Intermediate School and a trustee of Llandovery College – at both of which he donated scholarships – as well as subscribing to the funds of Cardiff College and St. David's College, Lampeter.

As an active member of the Swansea Urban District Board, he took great interest in the Penllergaer Board School, opened in 1881. He visited the premises regularly to compare registers and attendances, and the family visited often to present prizes. On 18th May 1884 he visited the school and wrote in the annuals, 'found twenty in one lobby and eighteen in another. Stone floors, no fireplaces. Draughty and unsuited for winter. Classrooms are required'.

In Penllergare Sir John preserved excellent relations with his many tenants and was noted for his benevolence. At a shoot he would present his workmen with one or two pheasants. At least three men were employed in the Pheasantry and Sir John was known to have reduced the rent of a farmer who allowed a pheasant to nest undisturbed in his thatched roof.

On 25th August 1893 Sir John suffered a personal family tragedy. His eldest son, William Dillwyn Llewelyn, aged 25, the heir to Penllergare and the baronetcy, was killed by the accidental discharge of his gun while out shooting in Penllergare Woods. The occurrence was rendered more sorrowful by the fact that he was shortly to be united in marriage to the Hon. Miss Gwladys Rice, eldest daughter of the Right Hon. Lord Dynefor, at Llandeilo. The funeral took place at St. David's Church, Penllergaer, on 29th August. Two days later, on 31st August, Sir John's other son, Charles Leyshon Dillwyn Llewelyn, was married to Katherine Minna Venables, of Llysdinam, Breconshire, at All Saints' Church, Newbridge-on-Wye.

Between 1890 and 1910 rural Penllergaer became transformed into a thriving colliery community with the opening of the three pits, Garngoch Nos. 1, 2 and 3. Sir John allowed chapels to be built at Penllergaer for a nominal fee, and donated a parcel of land alongside the Sunday School to be used as a recreational ground for miners and their families.

Lady Llewelyn died in 1917, aged seventy-eight, and Sir John at Penllergare House, on 6th July 1927, aged ninety-one. His coffin was carried to Penllergaer Church by his faithful workmen. A simultaneous service was held at St. Mary's Church, Swansea. The church at Penllergaer was unable to accommodate the large number of tenants and others who desired to attend the funeral service. The road to the church was thronged with people from Penllergaer and the surrounding countryside, all of whom wished to pay their last respects to the man they had looked upon as their guide, philosopher and friend.

Malcolm Hill, C.Eng. FICE
An extract from *Penllergaer and the Llewelyns*

Private collection

Family group. From left, Lady Llewelyn, Charles, William, Gladys, Sir John and Gwendoline, c.1889

The Making of a Village

For over 500 years, records show the land surrounding the dwelling at the top of the hill overlooking the valley of the Afon Llan has been known as Penllergare. Historically, old estates kept the spelling first shown on their title deeds in spite of mutations, alterations and later, more linguistically accurate versions. Over the centuries, with prudent management and at least two fortuitous marriages (in one the only child of the adjacent Nydfwch estate married the heir to Penllergare!) the estate grew, eventually to some 9,000 acres, as well as land in Carmarthenshire and Breconshire.

From the time Lewis Weston Dillwyn brought his young family out of Swansea to live at Penllergare in 1817, to the decline of the estate after the death of Sir John Talbot Dillwyn Llewelyn in 1927, the Big House and its inhabitants had an increasing influence and impact on the growth of the local community.

At the edge of the estate to the north-west, was the important crossway between Neath (to the east), the estuary (west), Swansea (south) and Pontardulais (north). It was marked at the beginning of the nineteenth century by the Old Inn on one side and by a few scattered thatched cottages. During this time the hamlet was known as Cors Eynon. After coal mining began on an industrial scale in the area from 1843 onwards and the railway arrived, the emerging township became known as Lower Cors Eynon and eventually dropped 'Lower'. The newly-built railway station there was called Gorseinon. To differentiate between the two places – the village at the top of the hill became synonymous with the Dillwyn Llewelyn estate of Penllergare and took its name. In 1890 for the first time the church register, during the incumbency of the Rev. T. P. Lewis, acknowledged the celtic origins, and more correct spelling of, Penllergaer – 'the head of the camp of fortified earthworks' – which it has remained ever since.

From 1817, as the estate grew in importance it provided employment. At the north entrance a lodge was built, and nearby John Dillwyn Llewelyn erected new slate-roofed cottages to house estate workers' families. Some of these still survive both at Cadle and Penllergaer. Three other lodges were built on the new drive at Penllergare.

Opposite the Old Inn, in 1837 the foundation stone was laid for a 'Chapel of Ease' known as St. David's. Built by John Dillwyn Llewelyn on the western boundary of the estate at his own expense and expressly for the benefit of his family, estate workers and the local community, it became a parish in its own right in 1944. A parsonage was built opposite. Apart from Sunday worship the church became the centre for most of the leisure and social activities of the area for two

Private collection

St. David's Church
and War Memorial, c.1920

The Cross, Penllergaer, c.1920. The building on the right remains, the others were demolished to make way for the modern filling station and the A48 realignment

generations. The family at the Penllergare House were enthusiastic supporters and benefactors of concerts, choir and Sunday School outings, national celebrations, festivals, fetes and sporting activities.

Next to the church JDL built Penplas originally as a convalescent and retirement home for his employees. It has also been known over the years as Gorseinon Villa and Pemplas before reverting back currently to its original name. Later the house was lived in by the head-teacher of Gorseinon Board School, was occupied for a time by the estate land agent and, at the time of Sir John Talbot Dillwyn Llewelyn's death in 1927, was the home of his butler Charles Richards. Although it is said Lewis Weston Dillwyn started the first school on the estate at which family members taught, the first village school was founded by JDL at North Lodge. When pupil numbers increased it became the girls' school and the boys' department was moved to Ysgol Gamp, later to become the Post Office. Eventually when larger premises were required the North Lodge school building became the Sunday School, the village library and the venue for meetings, parties, talks and lectures. Later Sir John Talbot D.L. built the Drill Hall for the 5th Glamorgan Volunteer Rifles on the north-east corner of the crossways and, after some renovation in 1920, he gave it to the church when it was renamed the Penllergaer Club and Church Institute. He also provided a cricket field and pavilion between Home Farm and the village to indulge his own passion for the game and as a local amenity. The gardens and parkland were frequently opened to the visiting public, especially at daffodil and rhododendron time, and many charities benefited from the fund-raising occasions held at the Big House and in marquees on the lawn.

With the sinking of the Garngoch collieries to the west, Mynydd Newydd to the south and Tirdonkin on the east of the estate, Penllergaer became less of a rural and more of a mining village. With greater opportunities

Watercolour of the original Chapel of Ease (St. David's) by John Dillwyn Llewelyn, 1873

for employment in the mines, the steelworks and other industries the demand for housing increased; and as the population grew so the influence of the Big House on the neighbourhood declined. After the death of Sir John and the earlier removal of his heir Charles Leyshon Dillwyn Llewelyn, on marriage, to Newbridge-on-Wye, the estate was sold on in turn to the Bible College of Wales and Glamorgan County Council. Lacking any viable purpose, inexorably over the next fifty years it fell into gradual dereliction, the core eventually being bought back by Sir Charles Michael Dillwyn Venables Llewelyn after the war. Housing development has since obliterated Home Farm and some of Brynrhos; and the M4 motorway and newly created A483 have caused major alterations to the landscape.

However, in spite of many changes, the once tiny hamlet of Penllergaer which evolved from the estate that gave it the name, now survives as a bustling suburb of Swansea.

Jennie Eyers
2003

The Village – Setting the Scene

I was born at 'The Mount' Penllergaer in 1929. My first name is Ernald but for some reason I was always called Vyron and I still am. It was a time of upheaval and change. These were the last days of horse-drawn transport and it was outside our house that the horses were mounted after travelling up the hill for one mile from Gorseinon. The village was characterised by the Big House, the residence of the Dillwyn Llewelyn family, and the surrounding estate covered a large area of several hundred acres. The village was located at the crossroad of two major roads at this time, the A48 and the A484. The whole area was littered with steel works, collieries and sheet metal mills including galvanised sheet steel. There were also hot dipped tinplate works and galvanised steel production units at Gorseinon and Grovesend that provided employment for the villagers. They used to wear steel-tipped wooden clogs and it was a familiar sound to hear these on the feet of workers going to work at 5 or 6 a.m. John's Buses provided a service but many chose to walk the distance of one mile or so to save money. This was a time when pennies were important.

Private collection

*Mothers' Meeting, 1886.
A photograph taken outside the schoolroom at North Lodge.
Lady Llewelyn is in the centre of the middle row*

Sir John and Lady Llewelyn, c.1900

A unique and attractive feature of the village was the Beech Walk; two columns of ancient trees [*apparently most of them were elm*] running down the slope from St. David's Church almost to the entrance gates of Penllergare Mansion. The trees were a wonderful indication of the beginning and end of the seasons with their brilliant spring and autumn colours. The Llewelyns used this route to attend services at St. David's. They had specially reserved pews in the church marked by poles with the family crest on them. They were great benefactors of the Church and Sunday School and I was on several occasions presented with a book signed by Sir Charles Dillwyn Venables Llewelyn as a token for good attendance. I still have one of these books called *Black Beauty,* dated 1939.

E. Vyron Williams
2000

Origins

My father first came here in 1937. He was one of five brothers who owned a bus company in Gorseinon and eventually sold out to South Wales Transport. With his share he bought this place [*now the garage by the roundabout*] and he put his first pump on Swansea Road. At that time it was the main road. Then when the road layout was altered and no longer came out by the Church, he put two pumps on the new Llangyfelach road. This house was called the Old Coach House and was built on an orchard belonging to the Old Inn as was the Drill Hall next door that became the Church Institute. However, they were all owned at one time by the Penllergare Estate.

There was a group of us when I was a lad, who used to go 'down the woods' if it was fine after Sunday School. We would go past the summerhouse and terrace until we reached the long flight of steps that went down to the Waterfall. We would play in amongst the rhododendrons, fish and sometimes snare rabbits. We knew how to do it by making a loop with wire. I couldn't do it now but then it didn't seem to bother us.

Wynford John
in conversation, 2005

Penllergaer

The village area was named after the estate and was even spelt Penllergare until about 1890. The General Strike started locally in 1930 and it was apparent to all families in the village that there were hard times ahead. During this period all the villagers ran up a debt to local shops and it was known as 'hen count' old account. After the strike was over the debts continued to hang over the families in the village for

Ysgol Gamp, the Boys' School by Michael Thomas, Llangyfelach Primary School, 2005

90

Otter hunt at Penllergaer, 12th August 1928

some years as they were slowly and painfully paid off. Some of the shops had to close because their capital was used up. These were the times of soup kitchens and widespread poverty. To this background can be added the prevalence of diseases like polio, diphtheria, scarlet fever, rheumatic fever, pneumonia and the horrendous all-time killer of consumption. Tuberculosis was a destroyer in many different ways and families moved if they had a member with TB because people and suspicion isolated them. In some ways this prevented the further spread of infectious diseases in the village. Even children in the school play area (yard) were warned by their parents not to play with certain children. Some families were almost wiped out and there is testimony to this in the graveyard of St. David's.

E. Vyron Williams
2000

Growing Up in Penllergaer

I was born on the estate in a thatched cottage, Penderri Cottage, in Penderri Lane. It was roughly where the motorway service station is today. You could get to it two ways, from the Pontardulais Road or from the Llangyfelach Road. Originally the main road looped up there but I think it was straightened out at the beginning of the twentieth century because there were so many accidents on that bend of the road by the river-bridge. Now the Twyn is buried under the motorway and all that area has changed.

The Blackwell family outside Penderri Cottage, 1928

The annual Boxing Day Hunt met outside the Old Inn. Sir John was a great huntsman. Isaac Davies was the head gamekeeper and the hounds were kept in the kennels next to his house. The hounds were used for fox and otter hunting. I remember the otter hunts in the mid 1930s when I was a lad. They went all over the place but usually ended up at Lower Lake. They would send the hounds into the reeds around the edge of the

91

lake to flush the otters out. Lower Lake was a great place. All the village lads would go down there in summer when I was young. We used to swim off the old dam and practice our diving.

We always called Isaac Davies, Ikey, but not to his face! He lived at Keeper's Lodge. He had a fearsome reputation and all the village lads were frightened of him but I am sure he was quite nice really and only doing his job. There was one tale my dad, Reg Blackwell loved to tell. He was only a schoolboy at the time and was probably coming home from there when he came across Sir John and Ikey in deep conversation. Ikey's dog was a bit bored with all this chat and was beginning to misbehave, jumping up, barking and being excitable. Ikey pushed him away and shouted at him to get down several times and eventually, in exasperation, aimed the stick he was carrying at the dog, to give him a whack. Only it missed the dog and came down with a thud across the shins of Sir John, who let out a howl the dog would have been proud of, and hobbled away in a great deal of discomfort. Of course, this was all rather funny to a youngster and Dad used to tell this story for years.

Jim Blackwell
in conversation, 2005

Cottage Stores

'Ray' Johns ran Cottage Stores in the 1930s which was next door to our house, 'Cotswold'. The two are now merged into the one shop. Cottage Stores was an experience. It was lit by one sixty-watt bulb. When the bulb burned out and was replaced by another, people marvelled at the brilliance of the place. The centrepiece, and hanging from the ceiling, was a large bird-cage containing one irascible cockatoo that spoke. Bacon used to come complete with ribs. These had to be cut out before the side was put on the bacon-slicer. The same old rusty knife was used for this, time and time again (and then, after a quick wipe on the apron, used to cut butter off the block). The bacon-slicer, even though constructed of chrome and vitreous enamel, was a boon to those inhabitants who couldn't stand things that glinted. I can't recall anything, ever, being washed. If the Medical Research Council ever does an investigation into digestive immunity they will find that the old customers of Cottage Stores are immune to everything. The contrast with Cross Stores was startling. Nevertheless, I was fond of her. I was OK for extra sweets – even more so when George Williams, of Llwyn-yr-Eos, who didn't eat sweets, gave me his coupons.

Don Maddox
2004

Margaret Bevan

Such a lot can be said about Margaret. She was one of the eleven children of William and Hannah Williams. Having a poor upbringing must have had its effect on her, as she eventually became a very

Margaret Bevan

Llwyn-yr-Eos being re-thatched.
George Williams is at the door

shrewd and efficient businesswoman. She ran the Cross Stores in Penllergaer village and was a moneylender of some repute, apparently claiming people's furniture if they didn't have the cash for repayments! When the estate sold off some of the tenanted farms and cottages, Margaret bought several properties including Llwyn-yr-Eos for her brother George to live in.

Alison Pullen
2005

My Grannie was Margaret Bevan. She had three children – two daughters Gladys and Nona and a son, Lewis, who became a vicar. She had a sort of smallholding and before she opened the shop in the morning she had already milked five cows by hand. She used to sell the milk to Charlie Jones. He was one of Sir John's chauffeurs and after the estate was sold up he became a milkman. My mother Gladys used to buy milk from him when we lived in Swansea Road, really to give Charlie a living. He'd come round on a bike with the churn and then ladle it out. It always amused my mother that she was buying the milk from Charlie from the cows *her* mother had milked that morning.

Jeffrey Phillips
in conversation, 2005

Auntie Maggie owned Cross Stores although in fact she lived in this house opposite at one time. Apart from being a cute business woman and a hard worker, she was also something of an apothecary. Whatever ailment anyone had she had a cure for it. She made up poultices and lotions and apparently was very good at diagnosing ailments and prescribing a remedy. Whether this was sheer intelligence or old country lore, I don't know, but it seemed to work. When I was a child I fell on an electric fire and got badly burned across the face from the bars. Auntie Maggie stayed up all night with me putting lotion on my face and a week or so later, when I was back on my feet, there was not a mark to be seen.

Wynford John
in conversation, 2005

George Williams

George was Sir John's huntsman who also did some gamekeeping and was by all accounts a bit of a womaniser! When Sir John Dillwyn Llewelyn and his entourage went off to France, ostensibly on horsy business, George used to go too. Whatever the business was, there was always time for socialising and time to entertain the ladies.

Alison Pullen
2005

Originally built as a drill hall for the amalgamated 3rd and 5th Glamorgan Volunteer Rifles, it was given by Sir John to the Church and became the Church Institute. It has now been replaced by the Llewelyn Hall

There was a story my mother told, that soon after their arrival in Penllergaer Sir John drove around the village in his brougham. The assembled villagers if women curtsied as he passed, and if men doffed their caps and bent their heads. "Not that you'd find me doing that" said Mother. A large percentage of the village worked in the Big House as ostlers, gamekeepers, gardeners, cooks and parlour maids. They had arrived from all over the UK to do so: Cambridgeshire, Pembrokeshire etc. In typical Welsh fashion they were known as Gladys the Cook, Thomas the Ostler, George the Groom. The latter had had a colourful life. The (never denied) rumour was that he had gone to Russia pre-1914 to look after the Tzar's stables and had married a minor member of the Russian aristocracy there. For whatever reason he returned to Penllergaer without her and took up his position with the Llewelyns. He lived at Llwyn-yr-Eos.

Don Maddox
2004

My mother said that a Frenchwoman once chased George all the way back to Pen-llergare. She probably thought George was landed gentry like Sir John. Poor woman she must have had an awful shock when she saw his little thatched cottage. Nowadays of course a thatched cottage is considered to be a bijou residence and is much sought after, but then it was something you couldn't wait to get away from. Llwyn-yr-Eos was very primitive with its *tŷ bach* at the end of the garden. Not at all ooh la, la!

Jeffrey Phillips
in conversation, 2005

Dear Mr. Maddox   30th January 1938

[from the correspondence between W. T. Rosser and A. J. Maddox]

I am sending you a rough statement of conditions as they were at the end of the 19th century in Penllergaer or to give it its proper name, Gorseinon, as often told me by my father, so I'll just get down to some explanatory items for you.

Penllergare House is, and always was, spelt Penllergare. When the Rev. T. P. Lewis was made Curate of St. David's (he came from Gorseinon) he started the Parish Magazine and realising the confusion of names that would occur, he arranged with Sir John to change the name of the village to Penllergaer.

I well remember the place being called Gorseinon and the present Gorseinon was called Lower Gorseinon. On the stone surround of the circular window of the day school you will still see Gorseinon Board School. It was the L&NWR people who called their station Gorseinon as a compliment to Mr. Llewelyn. Suggestions were made to call it Lewis Town and Rhyd y Mardy. It was from Mr. W. Lewis who owned Felyn Monach, a woollen mill, that they bought the land for the railway. These two names were turned down in favour of Gorseinon. This woollen mill worked as such until about 1888.

The 'Old Inn', Penllergaer was more popularly known as Ty Beddoe as the Beddoes lived there for over 200 years. 'Quarry Bach' or John Edwards was the great grandfather of the Reynish family and lived where David Francis lived for a time in a cottage (now demolished)

Sir John with Charles Richards as his loader, early 1920s

known as Tir Helig near the entrance to Coedwighywel Farm. When his coal level was last entered, about 1900, his pick and shovel were still at the face where he had left them.

Dear Mr. Maddox   24th May 1950

. . . Oh yes, perhaps you did not know that Miss Mary Vaughan (Post Office Terrace) has some 'Daguerre' portraits taken by Sir John's father whilst he and Fox Talbot were experimenting at Penllergare. I read in the Magazine the account of the funeral of Edward Williams, aged 90 years. He was the gardener at Maes y Gwernen, Morriston. I knew him as Ted Williams and he married Lizzie Stafford, daughter of Mr. Stafford, who lived at North Lodge. She was an excellent musician with the piano and could also play two tin whistles at the same time. It was she who taught us kids in the Band of Hope of those days and also organised concerts for the Sunday School outing. When we returned home, in the dark, instead of singing 'Hold the Fort for I am coming' we sang

Hold the Fox, for I am coming,
See the Hunters run.
Dai the Bryn & William Rosser
Jim and Mr. John.

I dare say you remember Dai the Bryn – Owen Bevan's father. William Rosser was my father, Jim was Jim Richards the Groom, and Mr. John was Sir John as he became afterwards.

Gorseinon Road, Penllergaer looking towards the Cross, c.1920

And with reference to bananas, Sir John told me that the banana plant at Penllergare was brought there from Dynevor Castle when he, Sir John, was a boy of seven. It was the first time he had seen bananas.

W. T. Rosser

Sales and Purchases

At first I thought the Bible College leased Penllergare from the Dillwyn Llewelyn family but they obviously bought it around 1940, because later on they started selling off some of the smaller properties. Mrs. Jones was leasing Home Farm at the time and she was able to purchase it. Keeper's Lodge was sold and so were the Gardens and Lower Lodge. That was the time my grandmother bought the two other lodges and then bought Llwyn-yr-Eos and Penplas. She left Penplas to my mother who later sold it. I believe North Lodge was given to the Church and afterwards they sold it to Phyllis Nozicka whose family, the Vaughans, had previously lived in it for years. Her father John Vaughan worked at Penllergare for seventy years. He started there when he was nine.

Jeffrey Phillips
in conversation, 2006

Rites of Passage

I was thinking the other day, about the rituals associated with the Penllergaer community, viz. birth, marriage and death. I can't say much about the first since it didn't make a lot of impact on us kids. We didn't notice if women were pregnant but were fairly familiar with the birth of lambs and calves.

Private collection

Melin Llan Bridge. demolished in 1976

Death made an impact, not just because it threw our timetable of play completely out of joint ("Nobody's playing outside while there's a funeral"), but because the solemnity of the occasion would wash over us. And it was a sad and solemn Occasion. The village had its undertaker/joiner, Clason Edwards, who lived in the house on the corner of Llangyfelach Rd. and Pontardulais Rd. and was a very good looking man. At least the village women classed him so. I think he played cricket for the village team. His main functions were to provide the coffin, dig the grave, arrange timings and bearers, etc. Each 'region' of the village had a few women who could 'lay out'. I know that my mother was one. One evening she was going out.

Wendy and Clive Edge outside the schoolroom at North Lodge

"Where are you going, Mam?"

"To lay out Mrs. Thomas with Mrs. Jenkins".

"What's that mean?".

"To see that she's washed and clean and peaceful".

"Oh".

The deceased was kept in the house. On death all front curtains of all houses were drawn. This was different. All the way up to the church there wouldn't be a naked window. It was permissible to peep between the curtains as the cortege passed. It didn't matter if one was young or old, whether it poured or was brilliant sun, the solemnity and dignity, gripped. Clason Edwards would lead the procession followed by the coffin, borne on the shoulders of six bearers. Every hundred yards or so there would be a halt to change bearers. Behind would come the mourners. It was very personal and very quiet, except for the tread of shoes. If anyone was, accidentally, caught outside they would stand, facing the procession, hats off if men, with heads bowed. There wasn't much in the way of traffic but the odd car had to wait. This was more important than someone getting to Port Talbot in half an hour.

Of course, women didn't attend. They stayed at home surrounded by lots of other women. In retrospect this ban on women was cruel. But at the time it was accepted. From what I can gather a lot of communal weeping took place in the house. I know mother would come back red-eyed and sniffily at such times. Perhaps it played some sort of function.

I think that the first use of a hearse in the village was when Mr. Jenkins, Llety Newydd, died towards the end of the war. Mother and I were in the front room and she said, "Mr. Jenkin's hearse shouldn't be long now."

I asked, "Has his horse died as well?"

Don Maddox
2004

Outings

The Sunday School was in the schoolroom at North Lodge in the 1920s. In the summer we would have wonderful outings. We would go on one of Mr. John's buses to Pontlliw and then by train to Aberavon Sands. Everything was provided by Sir John. One year there would be a trip for all the children and the following year a tea. There would be lemonade or tea, and lots of cakes. One I didn't like at all was seed cake – but there was fruit cake and buns too. After the food we would have games on the grass opposite the Lodge. As a treat I remember about six of us at a time were allowed a ride in one of Sir John's big cars, down the drive to Cadle, then round and back up the Swansea Road. One year we had a fairground but only once, because they ruined the cricket field. My two brothers were in the cricket team. They often played opposite teams of proper players who were invited to stay at the Big House.

The best Sunday School tea was at Christmas. There would be a wonderful tea sent over from the mansion. Sir John would sit in a chair next to the Christmas tree and he would present book prizes to every child. We were all invited to pick a gift off the Christmas tree and were given an orange.

My dad was employed as a gardener. They grew all the vegetables and fruit for the family in the Walled Gardens. When they had dinner parties with lots of guests my mother would help out with the food. Wonderful dinner parties they were. The gardeners also kept up the roads on the estate, they weren't tarred like today, but cobbled and had to be kept clean from weeds and the paths raked.

Edwin Anthony
*[From a recorded interview with Jennie Bowen,
Penllergaer Primary School project, 1977]*

Private collection

*Penllergaer Cricket Team with Sir John in the centre and Charles and Gwendoline either side.
Idris Edwards is the young scorer, not in whites, sitting on the ground, c.1920*

Family Connections

My family have lived in Penllergaer for years and years. I was born and bred here. Both my uncles on my mother's side, the Edwards, were involved with the estate. Clason Edwards was a carpenter by trade and after he came out of the army at the end of the war he set up on his own. At that time Keith Richards, of Rees Richards & Co., was the land agent and up here quite often (he had an account at our garage) and gave a lot of work, especially on the tenant farms to Clason. He was quite busy renovating barns, putting in new doors and generally improving properties. Clason was also involved with the hounds and the hunt. There were huge kennels just past Home Farm at the entrance to the Gardens.

Another elderly uncle of mine, Idris Williams, was one of the captains of the cricket team. Of course Sir John was mad keen on cricket and although it was the village team he had a lot to do with the running of it. Clason's brother, Idris Edwards, was the young scorer for the team. He must have been about thirteen or fourteen years old at the time. He didn't get paid anything but Sir John gave him the rights to fish on the River Llan wherever he liked. This was quite a reward because the gamekeepers normally wouldn't have allowed the village lads anywhere near the river as they would have supplied the village; and probably did!

When he was a bit older, Idris attended the Art College in Swansea for a while, but the war interrupted his progress and he was attached to the 8th Army Tank Corps as a driver/mechanic, and served in Egypt. Although he survived he never returned to art in a professional way, even though he was very good at it. Times were hard and he had to earn a living and after various mechanical engineering jobs he finished his working life at the tinplate works at Velindre, but after he retired he got out his sketchbook again. He died in 1995 at the age of eighty-six.

Wynford John
in conversation, 2005

Private collection

Penllergare House. Watercolour by Idris Edwards, painted from memory in his later years

Kotalko

I suppose all woods can throw up death stories. And Penllergare has its share. My godmother Rachel (Ray) Johns's husband, Charlie – who was something to do with the estate, shot himself, accidentally, when he tripped over a log with his gun unbroken and pointing in the 'wrong direction'. There were witnesses.

His mother, 'Old Mrs. Johns' was at one time licensee of the Old Inn. On retiring she oscillated between her daughter's place and relatives in Blackpool. She had a penchant

From l. to r. Mrs Phillips (Brynrhos Farm), Rosa Phillips, Mrs Johns (Cottage Stores) and Mrs Johns (Old Inn)

for the gee-gees and appeared to make money out of it. She was in our house one day when Mother had just washed her hair and said she thought it was getting thinner. It was throwaway remark. 'OMJ' said she knew of something to rub in the scalp but couldn't remember the name, but it would come back to her. The conversation got round to horseracing and what a lucky week the old girl had had. Mother said she'd love a certain tip (but had never placed a bet in her life, even though the village had a bookie's runner). 'OMJ' disappeared to Blackpool the following day and the next week my mother received an envelope containing a single sheet of paper with 'Kotalko' written on it. She contacted the runner and put 2/6 (a lot of money) on this horse. Later, he turned up at the house saying there was no such nag. Of course, it was stuff to rub on the scalp!

This story had a wide circulation for the Johns's were related to 'Daisy Clydach' who married Leo Abse MP, brother of Danny. I ran across the former a few years back and he was familiar with the 'Kotalko' episode.

Don Maddox
2004

Friends

[Delia June Thomas is the sister of Vyron Williams and lives in New Zealand]

After Christmas in the 1930s and 40s the weather seemed to get colder and I would awaken to a pale glow in the bedroom which indicated that snow had fallen overnight. On one particular bad winter the snow began to melt and then froze again. This was then topped by a fresh layer of snow. The resulting surface was extremely slippery and I practically had to crawl home from school. I loved to look up into the falling snowflakes as they touched my face so softly. Outside school hours I sought new paths of adventure. At the bottom of the garden where the hedge met with the garden shed was a gap big enough to wriggle through. At this point I would leave home and meet two boys close to my age, Stuart and Gordon Alexander. They lived with their mother and grandparents in an intriguing thatched-roof cottage in the nature of fairy tales. Deserting my dolls in favour of more boyish games, I would later arrive home in a happy state of grubby disarray. Blackberries beckoned in the field and hedgerows behind our house in late summer so we gathered them eagerly while we thought of delicious blackberry pies. During the cold winter months we played inside the cottage. Oil lamps were the only source of lighting. In the soft-hued surroundings, ghostly little shadows followed our movements. Water had to be carried in buckets from a supply at the end of a tree-lined lane leading to the road. A snowy-haired man, sole occupant of a room at the front of the cottage, would appear occasionally: 'Uncle George' as I knew him tolerated, but maybe didn't enjoy, the escapades of three little children in his autumn years.

Stuart and Gordon were the owners of an enviable accumulation of comics, *'Beano'*, *'Dandy'*, *'Radio Fun'* and *'Hotspur'*. In the honoured tradition of chief borrower, I arrived home on a regular basis with arms full. Books were a source of pleasure and enter-tainment in these long gone days before the advent of television.

Delia June Thomas
2000

Weddings

Brides walked to church. Instead of the closed curtains for funerals, people would be out on their fronts.

"Good luck, Gwenllian!"

And Gwenllian, Jean, Susan or Eirlys would always look radiant. This too was an Occasion. Surrounded by her bridesmaids, followed by mother and father, they walked up the middle of the road, happy, the genuine centre of attraction. Even us uncouth kids would remark, "Duw, doesn't she look pretty. Are you sure it's Peggy Morgan?"

Of course we didn't follow. Yet. We stood and watched in expectation. We had ulterior motives. When we heard that there was going to be a wedding there was one question that demanded an answer. It was a vital question. "Are they throwing money?" Sometimes they did. If they were we would, as soon as the bride and groom were in the church, congregate outside. A rope would have been tied across the open gates. Why did weddings last so long? Some kid, who'd done his homework, or was of a religious bent, would say, "Won't be long now boys. Last hymn."

The happy couple would emerge. We didn't give a toss how they looked. How many blue paper bank bags was the best man holding? One meant 120 pennies. Two, double that. Shared between twenty-five to thirty children. Not necessarily fairly shared. On one occasion the best man handed the groom a small shovel, such as one for removing ashes, onto which he emptied two bags of shining, mouth-watering, pennies. There were no sounds except the clink of coins and a lot of juvenile heavy breathing. Every eye was riveted to the groom's arm as it moved slowly downwards. Then a gasp as it jerked upwards, sending the cargo skywards. The pennies seemed to stay up for ever. Slowly turning and glinting in slow motion. All eyes are now wide, mouths open and the silence deafening. Then, like a winter squall, they rained on us.

If anyone ever wonders what it was like in ancient Rome when Attila and his mob descended they need look no further than Penllergaer church gates when they were 'throwing money.' It was mayhem. I know that my age-group friends were apprehensive about this particular bunfight. It was early in the war and there were an awful lot of Big Boys there. But I was satisfied. I managed to pick up 2d. John Heal and Gareth Thomas also had 2d each. We were rich. And the bruises and marks of hob-nailed boots on the back of the hands were fair prices to pay. The wedding party always found it highly amusing. No doubt the spectators in the Coliseum did too. Nobody was ever hospitalised. And no girls were allowed.

Don Maddox
2004

Changes

When I first came here in 1964 I think I knew almost everyone in the village. Now it has grown enormously and I don't know even half the inhabitants. It has expanded right up into the woods with a new village called Tircoed. Then in the other direction there is Parc Penllergaer that grew up in three phases on land that used to be part of Home Farm and Brynrhos. At the top of Swansea Road there is a lot of new housing also. The area has changed so much it would not be recognised by Sir John, his family or any of the previous generations who used to work on the estate.

Alma John
in conversation, 2005

Llwyn-yr-Eos with Hannah Williams and Aneurin David

Ty'r Ffald

No. 2, Tir Clement Cottages

Private collections

102

Pastimes, Games and Adventures

Skating

Lewis Weston Dillwyn's Diary.
Being Xmas Day a carriage load went to Llangyfelach Church and I remained all day at Penllergare. Frost very intense and in the afternoon John and Lewis skated on the Pond by the Farm.

25th December 1835

Amy Dillwyn's Diary.
Continued frost; beautiful day . . . Papa went shooting and only got three pheasants, one duck and a partridge. Mama, Harry, Llewellyn and I went over to Penllergare for skating and had capital fun there.

Elinor, Lucy, Willy and Arthur Crichton skated with us. Llewellyn and I walked and the other two drove.

Monday, 4th January 1864

Still bright fine weather with frost. Llewellyn, Harry and I walked over to skate at Penllergare again today and it was very jolly.

Tuesday, 5th January 1864

More frost. Mama and Minnie drove and the rest of us walked over to Penllergare and back today and skated all day . . . It is my 4th lesson in skating and I enjoy it excessively.

Wednesday, 6th January 1864

Path in the Upper Valley

Jennifer Cloke

103

Frost again. We all came over to Penllergare for skating. Mrs. Gulston and a lot of people staying with her came to skate also. I slept here [*at Penllergare*] tonight.

Thursday 7th January 1864

Cold and frosty as before. Returned home from Penllergare with Harry and Mama after skating all day. This afternoon we skated on the Lower Lake and I really think I am getting on.

Friday 8th January 1864

Thawed slightly and there was one little shower. I walked over to Penllergare . . . Elinor, Lucy and I skated all day though the ice was covered with water.

Saturday 9th January 1864

[*Harry was her brother, Minnie her sister and Elinor, Lucy and Willy were her cousins, the children of John Dillwyn Llewelyn. Llewellyn was her fiancé, soon to die of typhoid in Paris on the eve of their wedding.*]

I remember skating on Home Farm Pond. I also remember Dad skating there and falling over and breaking his nose. I don't have any recollection of Lower Lake ever freezing hard enough, probably because the river ran through it and moving water takes longer to freeze. Home Farm Pond was an excellent place to skate and often there would be as many as twenty or thirty people all out on the ice.

Jim Blackwell
in conversation, 2005

Amy Dillwyn's Diary

Intensely hot and very fine. Papa has bought the pony I rode on Tuesday and I have named him Rantoon. He seems a nice, quiet, surefooted creature. This afternoon Harry and I went over to Penllergare. He walked and I rode Rantoon. We stayed for dinner there and after dinner they tried to send up a fire balloon but it got set on fire for starting in the wrong place.

Amy Dillwyn, 13th August 1864

Our Gang

I had a wonderful childhood growing up at the Big House between 1927 and 1936. My girl friends came down to Penllergare House when their parents brought them. My brother's friends were allowed to come down on their own accord to play and, of course, I became 'one of the boys' – a real tomboy – doing as much as they did if I possibly could, but I was the youngest and the smallest and they looked after me. I suppose 'our gang' composed at various times of Leonard and Victor Williams, Harry and Jimmy Davies, Raymond Hughes, Elwyn Clement, Jimmy Blackwell and my brother and me. Later on when my brother went to Gowerton County school more friends came along. On more formal occasions my friends came down to play, the two Margaret Davies – 'Penlli' and 'Langy', Mary Davies, Nancy Blackwell, Peggy Tuxworth and Joan Howells. We were the ones who knew Penllergare the best.

Tableau Vivant, 1854. John Talbot D.L. (on the right), his brother William (front left) and their cousins, as directors of the Royal Amalgamated Railway Company. Photograph by John Dillwyn Llewelyn

There used to be great games of cricket and because the ball kept going over the railings we kept two stepladders handy so we could retrieve it. We climbed trees and also built a 'house' in a large tree between the tennis garden and the Drive. We had a wonderful 'speedway circuit' for our bicycles in the stable yard and I remember Victor Williams coming to grief when he fell and the scoop-shaped wire from his brakes went straight into his leg.

I remember my father talking to us all when the birds were nesting. In those days it was fashionable to collect different birds eggs, rather like stamp collecting. My father told us all we were never to go to a nest if we could see the bird in place because if she flew off, she might not return to her nest of eggs. We were not to take more than one egg from the nest however many of us wanted one for our collection and we were not to disturb anything but that ONE egg. One day when we were playing in the stable yard we found a Barn Owl's nest on top of the wall ledge under the loft roof. We were very excited and of course took one egg. We took it to show my father for we had never seen one before. He was so ANGRY that we had taken an egg from a Barn Owl. We said we would put it back! He was angry with himself, I expect, for not realising we would be thrilled at our 'find' and not think it was rare.

Betty Richards
2005

Gladys Dillwyn Llewelyn on her pony, c.1892

Ernald Vyron Williams when he was an intrepid explorer

Solo Expeditions

Hubert, who was detailed to keep a close eye on me, was a great brother to have and we had a pact not to tell our parents what he and his friends had been doing if I was allowed to follow him – at a distance. I was especially keen to know what Hubert got up to. I remember vividly my brother's friend hanging me over the Llan Bridge by my ankles and telling me if I dared tell my parents anything then the next time he would drop me into the river thirty feet below which was shallow and full of huge boulders.

My father built a round fishpond underneath a large horse chestnut tree. Hubert used to climb this tree to the very top. I tried it myself one day using a ladder to reach the first lower branch. He was very annoyed at this and told me that he would 'widdle' on me if I didn't go back down – and he did, and I fell into the fish pond below full of rotten leaves, worms, frogs and fish. I hurt my shoulder and had my arm in a sling for weeks. My parents told Hubert off but couldn't do it without a big grin on their faces. Very soon the whole episode was forgotten at home but most of the villagers knew about it because I told them that I had hurt my arm because Hubert had 'widdled' on me from further up the conker tree which brought about much laughter.

Hubert and his friends knew every track there was through the estate and I also became familiar with them. They ran for several miles along both sides of the riverbanks. On some of my solo 'expeditions' I would pick medlars and blackberries next to the Orchid House where one of my friends, Pat Edwards, lived. There were also some crab apple trees some thirty to forty feet high with large bright red apples but they were very sour. On the other side of the river valley towards Llangyfelach, there were several eating chestnut trees and I often collected chestnuts from these in the autumn. I would eat these raw and my mother warned me that I would have a bad stomach if I ate too many – and I did!

Some winter days I would get up early and go out on frosty mornings on some adventure wandering through the grounds of Penllergare entirely on my own. On my lone expeditions I would follow the paths and routes through all parts of the estate. I would even pay a visit to the Big House conservatory if the caretaker or gamekeeper were absent. But I never took

The River Llan in spring

The Waterfall

anything away for fear of upsetting Miss Vaughan. There was also an observatory, a tall round stone building with a spiral staircase. The top half of the building on the outside had wood cladding. I was unable to gain access to this building. It was firmly padlocked on the door entrance but there were some small windows through which you could see inside at the bottom of the building. It was many years before I gained access but by then it had been vandalised. Despite my trespassing, honesty was a must for me after being threatened by the venerable Miss Vaughan at Sunday School, who told me that above all things I must be truthful and honest or go to hell, and she painted a very grim picture of hell. This lady wore a black velvet ribbon around her throat with a cross or ivory brooch on the front. She was well respected in the village because she was a teacher at the church school long before the primary school was built in the 1880s. She had a hypnotic influence on me. My memories of her are real and vivid even today.

In summer I would make myself some sandwiches of home made jam and put them in a brown paper bag and depart at about 8 a.m. in the morning. My mother would be lucky if she saw me again before 7 p.m. in the evening – except on the days when my father was on morning shift. My time was spent in swimming in the Afon Llan with some other boys after damming it up with stone to form a deep pool and it was here at the age of about seven that I learnt to swim and stay underwater and dive. It was here that I was mesmerised by two parent snakes several feet long that were swaying their heads back and forth in unison with very beady eyes. I was petrified and hypnotised and couldn't move until they eventually slithered away. I think they were grass snakes and they had a clutch of eggs in a sawdust pile nearby which I found later. The eggs were round spheres, ivory white in colour, and all joined together in clutches. I always thought that these were a warning from Miss Vaughan to behave myself! It worked for several weeks and I did everything that my mother told me to do. I even cleaned the brass and silver, ran errands to John's shop with a note to do some shopping. At the same time as being a disciplinarian Miss Vaughan was a very loving person and helped many families in the village in practical ways when help was needed. On my frequent visits to Penllergare I would take note of the beautiful rhododendrons and azaleas around the place and as a peace offering I would take home a bunch for my mother. Sadly, the peace offerings were many!

E. Vyron Williams
2000

Hunting and Shooting

The Penllergare foxhounds were a well-trained pack and were at the Kennels just beyond the Home Farm. In the 1930s Mr. Lancoath was the Master of Foxhounds. He was then Town Clerk of Swansea and an excellent horseman. He had some wonderful horses, one I remember particularly for he could ride it up and down the flight of steps going from

Jeffrey Phillips

Lower Dam and cascade, c.1960

the front drive up to the gardens. We used to walk following the hounds for miles. One other occasion Mr. Lancoath's horse got into a bog the other side of the river and although everyone tried to keep it calm it was right in with its belly resting on the ground. Men carried doors taken off their hinges to lay either side and eventually they managed to winch it out.

The shoots at Penllergare continued whilst we were there and Isaac Davies who lived at the Keeper's Lodge would breed a lot of pheasants. This would be as well as hares and rabbits and, of course, pigeons and ducks. It was always a busy time when shoots were large, as 'beaters' had to be employed. I recall one occasion when an exhausted person arrived asking for a telephone call to be made to the doctor, as there had been a shooting accident and someone had been shot in the buttocks. He was carried to the house on a field gate that had been taken off its hinges and the doctor was already at the house when he arrived.

Sir Charles's elder son was in the Grenadier Guards and when he was studying for exams for promotion he came to live at Penllergare so we got to know Michael very well. A little later on his good friend Norman Gwatkin, also studying to become a major in the Grenadier Guards, came and stayed at Penllergare for peace and quiet and he, too, was great fun. Just before he left he took my parents, brother and me to the Plaza,

Chris Cray

the new large and glossy cinema in Swansea, to see the film 'The Maid of the Mountains.' George Llewelyn, Mike's younger brother, also came to spend time at Penllergare when he was studying for his engineering exams. Penllergare House was well used over these years by the Llewelyn family.

Betty Richards
2005

Lower Dam today, cut off from the lake and river and in ruins

Blind arch beneath the Drive

Marvellous Times

For several years in the 1930s, when in our early teens, a group of us lads would go quite often to Penllergare. We would go in the early afternoon of a weekend and get back by dusk. I always had an amazing sense of happiness whenever I was there. Even though only a youngster I was impressed by the beauty of the place. We had marvellous times swimming in Lower Lake. That was the main draw being able to swim there. Often we would swim to the island from the dam and that was quite a feat for a thirteen or fourteen year old as it was some distance. Sometimes ropes were attached to a big oak tree near the lock gates and we would swing out, higher and higher, and then drop into the water. It was all such fun. If we got cold we gathered wood, lit a fire and sat around. On one occasion we left it rather late to get home, it had got dark and we took a wrong turning through the trees. My father and my uncle came to look for us. I remember, to appease my mother, I picked a bunch of what I think was French Honeysuckle. Whatever it was, it was highly scented. When I got home there was a bit of a row.

D. I. Hughes
2005

Dai the Fisherman

When I was a youngster in the 1950s I was passionate about fishing. My parents promised me I could stay overnight at Lower Lake fishing when I was ten years old but I must have asked them first when I was six. I wasn't allowed there on my own. So I waited until my tenth birthday and first thing in the morning I was packed up and ready to go. I just couldn't wait. I think they allowed me over that day but not to stay – it was 1st January!

I fished off the dam mostly. The water was deeper there. My fishing tackle was made up of things I could find, bits of line left by other anglers, the rod from a tree branch and hooks I either found or made myself. The river and lake were teeming with fish;

mostly natural brown trout and I always caught something. Some I'd eat there and then, the rest were taken home for the family.

In the summer with the other lads that fished we'd get a pair of old shoes and nail planks of wood to the soles. The we'd wait until the lake dried up a bit and walk across the mud to collect the lines that had got caught in submerged tree trunks. In this way we collected our equipment for the next fishing season.

When I was thirteen or fourteen we lost the lake. I was there the day they breached the dam. It was only a small hole at first and we could jump backwards and forwards over it. Then it got wider and deeper and the fish swam through and into the river but we didn't mind at first because they were easier to catch. I don't know why they drained the lake. There were rumours of course. Some said it was flooding the mines, but the mines had closed by then or were on the verge of closing. It was an ecological disaster because they destroyed not only thousands of fish but also everything else that was living in that water. Velindre Steel Works polluted the river several times too. On one occasion in the 1960s it wiped out everything, the otters, kingfishers, dippers, the plant life as well as all the fish. It was a bad time and what was worse, there was nothing we could do about it.

David Whitelock
in conversation, 2006

Exploring

It was about a year after the Americans left (probably about 1945), when my pal, Vicky Walters, and I went exploring up at the Big House. We hadn't got quite as far as the mansion when, in the gardens, we found a large shaft about ten feet square going down about eight or nine feet. It may at one time have had metal railings across it but these must have rusted off. We jumped down and found a tunnel leading off that headed towards the house. We were able to walk along it as it was about four feet ten inches high and we were only small. At the far end we came across some rooms on either side. By this time there wasn't much light but we found a flight of stone steps leading upwards to a door. Obviously it hadn't been opened for a long time because it creaked horribly and scared the pants off us. There in front of us, in the gloom, was the biggest staircase I had ever seen. At least eight people could have walked up it side by side. We were staring at it when we heard a loud noise upstairs which really frightened us. Standing in the dim interior we were now convinced the place was haunted. We fled towards the big front door, that fortunately opened, and legged it down the drive until we ran out of breath. We never went back.

Haydn Davies
2005

The Best Days

Penllergare has been my life, my whole life. This is my valley. Even when I moved away for thirteen years, I always came back here. I never got to know the Clydach area – I would bring my dog back here to walk because this was my place. When I was in my mid-teens and had left school, me and my gang built a log cabin down here in the

Lower Lake. A smaller lake was reinstated on the site of the original in 2002/03

woods. It was a proper sort of place and there were six of us and we lived there for two winters and one summer. You'd never be allowed to do it now. The police couldn't understand why we wanted to live in the woods. They'd turn up every other night or so looking for gas meters. They had this thing about gas meters! Why on earth would we want gas meters there was nothing to spend the money on in the woods and besides we were working, we had enough. The first cabin got burnt down. Some said the police did it or it could have been other children, but we still stayed there. One night it was so cold we decided to build another place because all the shelter we had was a bit of canvas we nicked from a lorry that was parked up by the Midway Café. We went to work from there, in our fatigues, a gun over our shoulder, guitar in hand and maybe a rabbit or pigeon in our pocket. The boys in the tool-room at Mettoys called me Davy Crockett. We lived off the woods for more than eighteen months. There were rabbits, pigeons, and fish – if we didn't catch anything we lived on baked beans and Mars Bars – and occasionally we would buy a chicken on a Friday night. They were the best days of my life.

Although there were only six of us in the log cabin, other friends came down to see us when we were there. One evening there was about sixteen of us and there was an almighty electric storm. The thunder and lightening were virtually overhead and in the middle of all this a policeman turned up at two o'clock in the morning, absolutely soaked he was. He looks around and on one side we had our guns leaning up against the wall and the cartridge belts on hooks above and in the corner sitting down was one of our mates dressed in fatigues. Well, he goes over and looks down at him and says "And who do you think you are, Robin Hood?" This fellow, Ronald Dobbs was his name, gets slowly to his feet (we were all standing around holding our breath) and looks down at him and replies "I know you, you were in the Bs when we were at school and you hadn't much sense there either". Five minutes later we had this police fellow making seventeen cups of tea!

David Whitelock
in conversation, 2006

Chris Cray

Camellias outside the Orchid House in the Walled Gardens

Our Place

It was during the war, I was about thirteen or fourteen and my gang of friends and I played in the woods all the time. It was our place. We swam in the lake, out to the island and back, climbed trees and skimmed stones. Once we found an old punt, half-submerged, hidden in the rushes on the east-side. After some effort we managed to drag it out, clean it up a bit and float it. We made oars from branches and paddled around the lake for hours. It was wonderful. We were sailors, we were explorers, we were pirates! A few days later we returned to continue our adventure only to find the boat, where we had secured it, had gone. We searched all over and eventually discovered where it was. Obviously, some other lads had found it and pushed it over the dam. Our boat lay smashed at the bottom of the waterfall.

Haydn Davies
2005

The Mansion Den

When we were kids and it was raining too hard to be in the woods, the gang and I would go up to the mansion. To begin with the house was still standing and we would just walk in and wander from room to room. At that time we were collecting old bottles, Victorian ones, anything which we could sell for a few pennies. Later on when the place had been blown up we could still get into the cellars by crawling through the rubble. There were many arched rooms and in one there was a big safe with an iron door. The remains of the mansion were on top of us and we made our dens inside and lit fires. Passers-by would see smoke coming out of the ruins.

Sometimes we would have a bit of food with us for the day; tin of beans or something, everything else would come out of the river. We would throw a line in and pull out a trout. Then all you needed was a handful of dry ferns, light them and throw on the trout. By the time the ferns had burnt the trout was cooked. It might have been a bit burnt on the outside and a bit raw on the inside, but it didn't matter – it was fresh, it was beautiful and better than nothing.

David Whitelock
in conversation, 2006

Penllergare Goes to War

A Wartime Childhood

Penllergaer, the village, in the 1930s, was small, about 600 inhabitants, and with a good collection of old, thatched cottages facing the common. My parents came to live there shortly after their marriage.

During the war the Big House was occupied, in sequence, by the British and then the Americans. The appearance of soldiers in the village was a boon to us children. We were very impressed by the precision of platoons marching crisply down Gorseinon Road. We soon had our own army with its hierarchy and subsequent 'battles' between the top half of the village and the bottom. During this period Swansea had its blitz. The village escaped except for a stick of bombs that fell towards Pontlliw. The craters were solemnly inspected and shrapnel collected. One night there was an enormous explosion that shook houses and rattled windows. A parachute mine had come down and detonated on the other side of the valley down towards Cadle. The effect was similar to a minor meteor strike. Trees were cut off at ground level. Unluckily for the rooks it had landed right in the middle of a rookery. I recall George Williams walking down the road with a mass of rooks tied together. He gave my mother three. She, of farming stock, plucked, drew them and made a pie. None of us ate more than a mouthful. It was terrible. She soldiered on, finished her plate, said it was delicious and we were silly, but she wouldn't bother making it in future.

Then the British left and the Americans came. What struck us forcibly was the imprecision of their marching. They slouched. One, without a word, would break off the head of the column, dash into Cottage Stores, buy a loaf, catch up with the column and munch away. We were staggered. But there were compensations – rides in jeeps, chewing gum and lots of blissful Hershey Bars.

Don Maddox
2004

Mothers' Union 'Needles Poised', outside the Church Hall, Penllergaer, c.1940

Private collection

Air-Raid Wardens at Penllergaer, c.1940

An Encounter

When I was a lad I met two American soldiers on the Drive near the mansion.

"Where can we get a cup of tea and a snack around here?" they asked.

"Nowhere on a Sunday," I replied.

They looked at each other in horror.

"My Mam will give you some tea," I said. "Wait here," and I ran home to Fforesthall. Mam got a thermos flask ready and back I went (at least a mile).

The Yanks were still there and were they grateful! I was given a note for my trouble. I didn't realise the value, it could have been foreign money, I'd never seen a white £5 note before.

When I took the money back to Mam she was quite stern and said we weren't to keep it as it was only a flask of tea and a packet of biscuits she had given. I was to return it. So, back I went up the hill (more slowly this time as my legs were tired). The Americans quite understood and gave me some coins instead. Mam seemed to think that was alright.

Haydn Davies
2005

Reg and Jack

Reg Blackwell and my father, Jack Maddox, were good friends and went back a lot of Penllergaer years. Fortnightly they used to cut each other's hair. Monday evenings it was either Annie at our house or mother at theirs. In 1927, according to Dad's diary (he was an inveterate diary writer) they all spent Christmas with the Blackwell parents. Reg's father Arthur was from around Essex or Cambridgeshire, and was a gamekeeper on the estate. On retirement he went back to Castle Camps, where he died. The Blackwells were also related to the Elsdens of Melin Llan.

During the war and the Redirection of Labour, Reg and Dad, with others, were posted off from the Grovesend Tinplate works to ICI in Birmingham. In the long term this was a good thing; non-contributory pensions, skilled craftsmen, training, etc. After a few years they were posted back to the new ICI plant at Waunarlwydd. They were coming home from Brum one Christmas. The train passed Landore and was coming into a blacked-out High Street Station. Reg stood up, stuck his ticket in his mouth, his trilby on his head and grabbing his two suitcases went to the door. Peering out he said, "We're there boys", opened the door and stepped out. Into a void. The train was still moving slowly and not near the platform. When it did stop they all rushed back to find Reg walking up the ramp at the end of the platform, his trilby on his head, his ticket in his mouth, a suitcase in each hand, but looking as if he'd spent a week at the coal face while wearing a shredded raincoat.

Don Maddox
2004

Living at the Gardens

Private collection

Penllergare House from Beech Walk, 1939

I was born in 1939 at the outbreak of the war. My father was away on active service and I moved to live at the Gardens in 1942-43 with my mother and grandmother. Before that my grandmother lived at Coed Tremig but when my grandfather passed away she had to leave. There was no sympathetic attitude in those days.

I remember the way the glasshouses were laid out and I distinctly remember the smell of the tomatoes growing in the greenhouses that were heated by hot water from boilers situated by the back door of the Walled Gardens. A large variety of produce was grown including peaches, of all things, growing against the inside wall.

The Americans were stationed in the mansion area. They used to travel to the lake near Cadle and put up a bridge over the lake. It astonished me that sometimes they would put it up during the night and take it down at daylight and then they would reverse the procedure. It was not difficult for a young lad such as me to observe them unnoticed.

Gerald Redman
2003

Private collection

Rustic footbridge in the woods, c.1850. Photograph by John Dillwyn Llewelyn

Morgan Pugh and Ikey

I can't recall the reason for my visit to the Big House under British occupation except that it was to take a message to someone. It was sentried and barb-wired. The interesting thing about the house was there seemed to be galvanised, smoking chimneys emerging from most windows. My visit could well have had something to do with Morgan Pugh. He was, it was said, a sheep farmer from the Eppynt. Why he ended up at Penllergaer is anybody's guess. I can see him now. A small, wiry man with a bald crown and a mane of white hair. More like a stereotypical evangelist than ex-sheep farmer. He rode a creaking bike and always smelled of wood smoke. He had taken up residence in what he called 'the lighthouse' but was, in reality, the decrepit Observatory. He did odd jobs for the military.

Although the House was pretty well guarded the grounds weren't. They were known as 'The Grounds'. "How about a walk around 'The Grounds'?" They were an ideal play area for us. Swimming in the Lower Lake (the Upper Lake was weed bound) and also in a pond above the old bridge at Melin Llan. The only, terrifying, obstacle was one 'Ikey' who had all the properties of Godzilla. He was a gamekeeper (even during the War) and what he did to trespassing kids was the stuff of frightening legend. Not that anyone had ever come across him. I don't know what Ikey's real name was. Somewhere at the back of the head is a feeling it could have been 'Isaacs', but I'm not sure. I'm equally unsure as to where he lived but think it was somewhere in the Forestry. His reputation would have made his dwelling a deep, underground cavern.

Don Maddox
2004

Before the Invasion

Most of the Americans lived in the Big House but there were also a few huts outside either side of the path that led to the Observatory. The ones up here in Penllergaer were mostly white, while down at Grovesend there was another camp and they were mostly black. Mum and Dad used to have some of them over for a meal. There was Johnnie, he was Maltese, or rather he was an American but his parents were Maltese. A lot of them came over to our house on a Saturday night. Then they all left suddenly just before D. Day. They seemed to disappear almost overnight.

An aperture in the garden walls

There were these two characters in Penllergaer Village at that time nicknamed Slim Jim and Tommy Amen. They were henchmen of Mrs. Williams, the Headmaster's wife, who was a devout chapel evangelical. They had a meeting house at the back of the lane behind our house on Gorseinon Road and as children we used to watch from the window, fascinated by the total immersions that went on in the pool. We didn't understand most of it as we were church and not chapel. Later on when I was a bit older, I got to know these two, and what was more important at the time was they had a CAR. I went down to the Bible College with them and was able to nose around and see some of the marvellous work that had been done to the Big House. The College people had decorated a lot of the rooms and painted beautiful murals on the ceilings, a bit like the Sistine Chapel. A lot of these were destroyed when the place was taken over by the military.

Jim Blackwell
2005

British Soldiers at the Big House

I remember the woods most of all because I did a lot of my courting there! There were British soldiers at the Big House first during the war because that's where I first met my husband, David Pember, because that was where he was stationed. Then after the British the Americans arrived. They made a big impact in the village but were welcomed. Of course they had lots of money (well, more than we had or so it seemed), they could get silk stockings and they had a band and held dances in the Church Hall. The British Army had a small group and had dances too, well more of 'sixpenny hops' but it was wonderful for the girls because so many of the village lads had been called up and had gone away.

Nancy Pember
in conversation, 2005

Chris Cray

Blocked doorway to Walled Gardens

Flightpath

During the war, the Cricket Field was used by light aircraft for a time. As a youngster I lived in Swansea Road and if we were playing in the garden and heard one approaching we would stop and watch. The field was really too short as a runway, especially for take-off, as the plane often had to pull up which caused it to somersault. The Yanks would then run out from the Big House, turn it up the right way and the pilot would try again. My friends and I were endlessly entertained by these antics and we were disappointed when the flights stopped. I guess they found a less expensive way of delivering messages.

Noel Phillips
in conversation, 2006

Jennie Eyers

The river in winter

Remembering

Death of Mr. William D. Llewelyn

News of the sad death of Mr. W. D. Llewelyn, accidentally shot in Penllergare Woods on Friday, 25th August 1893, has been received with profound feeling of regret by all cricketers, to whom he was well known as an enthusiastic follower of the game. Born in April 1868, the deceased first came into prominence as a member of the Eton College eleven. Proceeding to Oxford, Mr. Llewelyn's abilities at once claimed attention, and he played for his University both in 1890 and 1891, occupying the position of hon. sec. in the latter year. The deceased accompanied Lord Hawke to India last winter, and this season he closely associated himself with the cricket of Glamorganshire, for which county he was a J.P. Mr. Llewelyn's brother Charles was married only the day previous to the lamentable occurrence, and himself was shortly to be married to the eldest daughter of Lord Dynevor.

Extract from
'The Field' Book of Cricket, 1893

William Dillwyn Llewelyn (1868-1893)

William was Sir John and Lady Llewelyn's eldest son and heir. He was a great sportsman like his father and particularly loved playing cricket. He often used to bring a team from university to play the village team here and of course the local team always lost. William had a shooting accident in the woods, well that is what the family at the Big House said and what was reported in the press, but the local people knew something different. Everyone was talking about it and according to my Grandfather, he shot himself. He was in the search party when they found him and I think he said it was in the Quarry.

Jeffrey Phillips
in conversation, 2005

118

Tirdonkin

My grandfather on my mother's side, Dafydd Evans, worked at Tirdonkin colliery on the east side of the estate. He was the colliery fireman, who was responsible for all the safety aspects of the underground workings, and he died in consequence of an accident there. It was the end of a shift in 1939 and he was doing some rounds checking on things, when he saw two young miners struggling with a pit prop. Whether they were trying to prevent a fall-out from the roof, I do not know. But he went to their aid and he was the only one injured in the accident. He died later in hospital.

D. I. Hughes
2005

Looking Back

At the beginning of the twentieth century my mother was a maid at the Big House and my father was a thatcher by trade and travelled around quite a bit. He had to go where the work was, of course. Charles Richards, Sir John's butler, gave my mother away when they married and we were always very friendly with the Richards family. When Sir John was an old man and very ill, the only person he would have near him was Charles Richards.

When I was a youngster I would go up to Penllergare House to play with his two children, George and Betty. They used to invite us to their birthday parties at the Big House and we would play hide and seek all over the place. I remember the Round Room and Sir John's bedroom. He had a four-poster bed but I was also struck, even at a young age, with the bareness of the room. There was a mat beside the bed but no carpet at all, just bare floorboards. Mind you, the floors were made of very good wood. Even the back staircase that was only used by the servants was made from figured oak. I remember that at the top of the back staircase was Miss Llewelyn's dolls-house.

Private collection

Home Farm from Windyridge, Swansea Road. Watercolour by James Lamond, c.1948

119

The Richards children kept their toys and games in the Butler's Pantry. Once when we were in there George said to me "See that door? Well, give it a kick!" It looked like a perfectly ordinary wooden panelled door. But he kept on saying "Go on, give it a kick. Give it a hard kick" so I knew something was up. Then he opened it and it was made of steel and painted to look like wood. It was obviously the strong-room where they kept the table silver and valuables. It always puzzled me as to why they had two big lead-lined sinks in the Butler's Pantry. One explanation could be it was a softer surface for washing crystal and silver or, I wondered, if it was used at one time by John Dillwyn Llewelyn for his photography, for putting his photographs into chemical solutions.

Private collection

Towards Upper Lake.
Watercolour by Emma Charlotte Dillwyn Llewelyn

I worked in the Walled Gardens for a time when I first left school. It was in 1937. The Edge family were running a market garden. There was Sam Edge, he was the owner and he had two sons Tom and Willy who worked with him. There was a daughter [*Sylvia*] too but I think she was a bit younger. The Walled Gardens were very large and the Edge family grew quite a lot of vegetables but mostly they were interested in flowers. I was the gardener's boy and did a bit of everything. I worked there for about two years. The Bible College of Wales was doing the Mansion up and then the war came and everything changed. I then worked in a shop as an errand boy and joined the Home Guard before I was called up in 1942 and spent three years in India.

In 1961 we went down to watch the day they were blowing up the house. We were no more than half way when we heard this big bang and thought we were too late. But when we came to the house it was still standing looking just the same, we couldn't believe it. The army engineers had packed three or four charges into the wall of the inner hall thinking that would be sufficient to flatten the place, but all it did was blow a hole in the wall. They had a heck of a job pulling it down. It took them several weekends and on one occasion they brought in one of those armoured tanks and put chains around the walls and pulled them down. It was quite a performance.

Victor Williams
in conversation, 2004

Muriel Drinkwater

There was a sad event in 1946. Muriel Drinkwater, a schoolgirl attending Gowerton Grammar School for Girls, got off the bus at Melin Llan. It was a day of torrential rain. Between the Llan and her home at Tyle Du she went missing. The village and police formed many search parties and she was eventually found, halfway home and shot with a pistol. It was the first of 'notorious' child murders that are now commonplace. Fleet Street took over the village. Nobody was ever arrested.

Don Maddox
2004

Penllergare 1936-1949

'The Woods' were always part of my childhood: walks with my father every Sunday and once a duck shoot with him at the Lower Lake (where the army made a pontoon bridge during the war): sliding on the frozen pond at the Home Farm: picnics on the slope above the lake amongst bracken and bluebells: exploring the two waterfalls and the many flights of steps: expeditions with Annie for eggs: and always

Jennifer Woods (née Lamond) on the ice at Home Farm pond with her mother

rhododendrons. But the main playground for us children was the Scout Field in front of the Big House, a lush area covered with solid grassy mounds that our Welsh Terrier had to leap over in great bounds. We came in by the path off the road to the Home Farm at a hut (the Scout Hut?) under an oak that kept its leaves through the winter and dropped them in the spring (perhaps a Lucombe Oak). The dog would head straight for the old yew tree at the far side which was lined by yellow azaleas, bamboos, some fine conifers and of course rhododendrons. Opposite was a magnolia.

The yew tree was our domain, it spread its enormous branches from near ground level and the dog would venture on to the lower ones while we shinned higher (are there still initials up there?). We called it the 'King of Arms' and it was a castle, galleon, tank or mundane bus. It is still there, severely maimed by successive developers but a proud remnant of what once was.

I have since spent a happy career always amongst plants for which I thank those formative years. On my parents' grave in Blairgowrie in Perthshire reference is made to Penllergaer and a much-moved golden azalea from the Scout Field scents the air every year, both testament to a very happy sojourn in South Wales.

Jennifer Woods (née Lamond)
2006

Changes

There is a Chinese expression, 'you may be born in interesting times'. I was born at the beginning of the Second World War, so this probably qualifies as interesting! One only becomes aware of surroundings slowly. I was born in Swansea Road, Penllergaer, which at the time was just a finger of houses built in the 1930s; nothing remarkable, but across the road was Home Farm adjacent to the Penllergare estate. Obviously at the time I didn't think my environment was unusual. Mrs. Annie Jones lived in Home

Farm a close friend of my father's farming family so my brother and I could wander at will. To us it was a giant playground.

We would climb a series of steps, which took one over the ledge into Home Farm. In spring there was a carpet of celandines, purple violets and bluebells on either side. The estate criss-crossed by numerous bridle paths was still completely intact. Down we would wander below the Cricket Ground until we got to the Big House now empty and ever so slightly forbidding. The American Army had not long vacated the 'House'. At the time Mr. Brown the caretaker was careful that no intruders disturbed its slumbers.

Down we would go past the hundred steps and the giant Monkey Puzzle trees, the Drive clung precariously to the side of the valley eventually coming to the Upper Lodge, thence to open fields and finally Middle Lodge. Why I wondered had these Hansel and Gretel cottages been built in such lonely places? Outside Middle Lodge there was an upturned boat which must have been used on the Lower Lake. Through the trees could be glimpsed a gleaming expanse of water. As one got closer a torrent of liquid poured over the falls and roared as it dropped into the water. I'm afraid it made me faintly uneasy. Everywhere rhododendrons, some of breathtaking beauty, flourished, dark yellow azaleas released their heady perfume into the air. The acid soil of Penllergare was the perfect medium for growth.

This was the Victorian paradise of the Llewelyn family, now in rapid decline. Familiarity breeds contempt I suppose and only now in retrospect can one marvel at the extravagance and confidence of one extremely wealthy family which enabled them to turn this vast area into their own back garden from which everyone was excluded. I was witness to a changing social order. There was no longer a quiescent class of people prepared to work for nothing or next to nothing. Universal education, so resisted by the wealthy, had changed the social system. There was no more cheap labour or people grateful for a roof over their head. My maternal grandmother, brought up on the estate with a large family in the tiny, two bedroom Middle Lodge, eventually set up her own business in Penllergaer known as Cross Stores and she was determined to educate her children. My mother and her sister became teachers, their brother a vicar. Definitely a step up!

Chris Cray

Ornamental well or grotto in the remains of the rockwork garden, on the terrace above the Upper Lake (Fishpond)

The estate was a thing of beauty but like all estates could only function with the toil of the poor. I'm afraid my grandmother shed not one tear for its demise. "They had all the money. We did all the work", she said.

As a little boy I was taken through the empty shell of the mansion. The vast rooms where the family was ensconced were now gloomy and empty. Still functioning was Sir John's manual lift which took the aged gent to his bedroom. We walked out onto the balcony. I felt briefly like royalty. I do remember the kitchen ranges which were enormous, and the back of the house was a warren of servants' quarters.

A path in the valley

The war hastened the decline of this estate of course, and the house just crumbled. The then owners, the Bible College of Wales, had hoped to make it into a school, but requisitioned during the war, and finally owned by the County Council, there was little money in post-war Britain to spend on these mausoleums.

The final chapter came in 1947 when Charles Tyler the builder moved onto the Cricket Field. First to go was the awesome avenue of beech trees stretching from the Church to just below the Cricket Field, and roads were marked out. Charles Tyler became bankrupt before building started, and the estate was granted a temporary reprieve. Finally the prosperous sixties saw a huge rise in demand for homes and building began again in earnest.

A surprising amount of the grounds are still extant however, and surely should be preserved for posterity. There is still time, but developers are hovering and sadly the Llewelyn family seem indifferent to the land they still own. Let's hope this wonderful green space on the outskirts of Swansea can be saved for the benefit of everyone.

Jeffrey Phillips
2006

Times Past

My earliest memory of Penllergare is in 1955, when I was five. I was on a Sunday School outing with the Bible College of Wales. It was to be a mystery trip; there were about fifteen children, including my sister Dawn and my brother David. We were transported on the back of an open top lorry (we would not get away with that today!). We each had a cushion to sit on, it was very exciting. It seemed a long way but it was only from Derwyn Fawr. Our driver 'Uncle Toby' decided to park at the farm near the Walled Garden as this would be the shortest walk to the lake, but the farmer was not too pleased with this plan! He eventually agreed and we set off for the lake. Here we had our picnic and played games. I thought the lake was beautiful. There were late flowering rhododendrons and azaleas in the woods and I became a 'rhodoholic' from that day on.

A year later my family moved to Blaen-y-Maes. My Dad took us over the woods for a walk and you can imagine my delight when I found my beautiful lake again. Penllergare was to become my playground of delight, discovery and learning for the next ten years. I loved Penllergare House, we were told not to go in as it could be dangerous, but of course we went in anyway! We discovered the 'secret waterfall' my favourite place and several sets of stone steps leading to it. And the lovely stone bridge, alas, destroyed by vandals. Fortunately, Mother Nature and time covered most of the features and many have survived, waiting patiently to be discovered.

One sad Sunday in January 1961 the house was 'blown up'. We were not allowed near so we watched from across the river, all we saw was a cloud of dust. In later years the dam was removed from Lower Lake and my beautiful lake was lost. I roamed everywhere with my friend Glenys. We swam in the lake and the river, climbed trees and made secret dens. One day I lost my sandal in the mud on the edge of the lake, boy I got in trouble that day! As we got in our teens we did a fair amount of courting there as well.

Penllergare shaped my life. I never lost my love of plants and I now work in the plant centre at RHS Rosemoor. The magnificent rhododendrons have always been my favourites. I now specialise in them. I walk Penllergare every time I visit Swansea. I am so pleased the estate is being restored. It is a massive but worthwhile project.

Yvonne Colman
2006

A Place for all Seasons

Four generations of my family have been captivated by Penllergare. When I was a child my father (also named William) and I would visit Penllergare from the Cadle Mill end, once a year in December at night, in order to obtain our Christmas tree! He used to play and swim there when he was young after walking over from Townhill. Later, in the early 70s we lived just off Ystrad Road and with my friends I would go on day-long expeditions 'up the woods'. There used to be a little shop at Cadle Mill that was open on a Sunday which was unheard of in those days. There we would stock up on Fruit Salads and Blackjacks and maybe a bottle of pop (a luxury!) before heading up the west bank of the Llan and on to the dam of the drained lake. We never had the nerve to go any further up the valley and so the 'hidden waterfall' remained a thing of legend to me until many years later.

I rediscovered Penllergare in the 1980s with my son Paul and Jack Russell terrier Cai. Those were the years when I came to really appreciate Penllergare, to learn about its secrets and to truly revel in its tranquillity and natural beauty, so that now it has become a place of great spiritual significance for me. These days I regularly visit with my grandson Rhys and Cai's successor, Buzz. Rhys calls the place 'badger's wood' and the riverside route up from Cadle Mill is his 'secret path'. I like to think that for him Penllergare is becoming a special place that will also develop into a lifelong passion. It has fulfilled my needs over the different seasons of my life – a playground in my childhood, a sanctuary in my youth and a place of escape in recent years. I say to my wife that I'm off 'up the woods' and she knows exactly where I mean.

William Jewell
2006

Demolition Day at the Big House

I was about sixteen when the house was demolished in 1961. Three friends and I had been to St. David's Church on 15th January and afterwards, still in our 'Sunday best', decided to go and have one more look at the old house. We walked past North Lodge and managed to get down to the swinging gate but there we met a mountain of mud. Heavy TA vehicles had churned up the road and it was impossible for us to carry on.

We met a smartly dressed officer and I told him that as I had lived on the estate, I wanted to see the house one last time. He called over four young TA lads and told them to carry us to a place of safety. We were carried to the middle lawn facing the house. To the left of us was a heavily wooded area where the summerhouse had been. A large rookery had always been there and usually it was very noisy, but on that day not one bird could be heard. We just stood there and everything was silent. A hooter sounded and we heard a charge going off. For a long time nothing happened, then all of a sudden little wisps of dust appeared from cracks before the building just folded in on itself. It was the end of an era.

Beryl Brain
2004

Picnic in the ruins

Sometime in the early 1960s, with George's children Jennifer and David, we stopped off at Penllergare on our way to Gower and had a picnic sitting amongst the ruins of the Penllergare House. I wanted to show them the place where we grew up and after we had eaten we walked down to the Waterfall. Already the vandalism was apparent, branches had been ripped off trees, the iron fencing pulled up and a lot of stone from the walls had been taken away. But it still had the atmosphere of its elegant past even though its present was in ruins.

Betty Richards
in conversation, 2006

Quarry Bridge

Richard Morris

A View of the Future

Penllergare . . . is something brilliant waiting to happen but until someone takes some action it will remain neglected and grow more wild. It is one of the places that should be kept for eternity for everyone to share and cherish.

The Waterfall is beautiful. The water rushing down the rocks and then flowing into the long and winding stream is marvellous. The sound of the wildlife surrounding you is fantastic especially when it echoes in the tall, strong trees swaying in the wind. The thought that people used to live here is amazing, you feel as if you are standing on history. It was fabulous.

I certainly don't like the way the lake is all overgrown. There is even a little island in the centre full of plants. All the trees are bunched up and have taken over completely. I hated the big, ugly drainage pipe in the middle of all the beautiful scenery. It was like having a weed in a garden.

If I was making the decision on what should happen in Valley Woods, I would make it more modern but also keep certain features that make the woods special. I would probably turn the woods into a mirror maze. Instead of having mirrors for dead ends I would project photographs taken by John Dillwyn Llewelyn in his life. In the centre would be the Waterfall and surrounding it different pieces of information about the woods.

Jessica Hills
Year 6. Penllergaer Primary School, 2004

Jennie Eyers

Year 6, Pontlliw Primary School, 2005

In the Future

Penllergare is a wonderful place. It is a place to have adventures. It's a nice place to have a walk or to get some peace and quiet. In the future I would like to see a park for children to play in. I would like to see people doing fishing and I would like to see boats by the side of the lake to make it look like it did before.

I don't like the dumped cars or the stinging nettles. The cars make it look like a place where they have let off a car bomb. Also I don't like the broken steps. I don't think they are safe. I do like them being an original item of the estate but I would like them made safer.

Amber Bowers
Year 6. Pontlliw Primary School, 2005

Further Thoughts on Valley Woods

I would like to see the area cleaned up, the cars need to be removed and the graffiti cleaned off. I would like to see this area turned into a nature reserve where families could enjoy a day out. There could be picnic areas and maybe a coffee shop where people could sit and have a drink while enjoying the scenery. An education centre would be fun. This could be placed where we could go to learn about the plants and animals that live in the woods. We could also learn more about the history of Penllergare. But the building work must be kept to a minimum and must not spoil the natural beauty of the area.

Adam Lewis
Year 6. Penllergaer Primary School, 2004

Eloise Williams
Pontlliw Primary School, 2005

Keiran Meredith
Portmead Primary School, 2004

What We Can Do

Penllergare is a lovely place but there are some things that are not so good, like all the dumped cars that people have set on fire. There is also the Council Office that is in the same place as the mansion used to be. Now all the plants have overgrown, there are nettles everywhere and the steps are cracked and crumbling. In the future I think all the overgrown plants should be cut back so that people can see the lake. I also think the Council Offices should be knocked down and a copy of the Mansion should be built as a gallery for all the old pictures of Penllergare. I think the broken steps should be replaced with new ones and a fence put around the place so motor vehicles cannot get in.

Bethan Bedford
Year 6. Pontlliw Primary School, 2005

Ceri Richards
Llangyfelach Primary School, 2005

Ashley Bryant
Penllergaer Primary School, 2001

Ben Bennett
Pontlliw Primary School, 2002

Kirsty Northcote
Portmead Primary School, 2004

Thoughts to the Future

Eventually I found a space in the car-park, where the Big House once stood. Then across to the Observatory to ponder how it could fit in with our plans for Penllergare Valley Woods.

On the Terrace Gardens, along which I first scrambled fifteen years ago, I compared Ken Murphy's archaeological survey with the photographs of 150 years ago by John Dillwyn Llewelyn. Surely it should be possible to recapture the magic of his romantic design? Moving on I noticed that the rediscovered mulberry was showing signs of revival. Next to the Walled Gardens; despite the neglect and damage, restoration to demonstrate Victorian kitchen horticulture in its heyday seems both appropriate and feasible. In the ravaged lower valley I checked up on the work already in hand to transform it into a community woodland.

I finished my walk at JDL's waterfall, still a favourite haunt for children. Perhaps I'm perceived as unwelcome authority because one calls out, "This is our place!" "Yes", I reply, "then it's up to you to look after it".

Michael Norman
2006

Penllergare Valley Woods

When I go to Penllergare Woods
I hear the wild wind whistling,
I hear the waterfall gushing,
I hear the dry leaves blowing around my knees.

When I go to Penllergare Woods,
I see dragonflies all colours as bright as the sun,
I see an overflow of green grass upon the horizon,
I see clear clouds floating around the pale blue sky.

When I go to Penllergare Woods,
I can feel a tickle of the soft stem of a furry flower,
I can feel bark as rough as sandpaper,
I can feel pebbles as smooth as silk.

When I go to Penllergare Woods,
I can smell the musty smell of damp leaves,
I can smell a sweet scent of honeysuckle,
I can smell the lushest green grass.

Eryn Creed
Penllergaer Primary School, 2006.

Amy Thomas
Penllergaer Primary School, 2005

Rachael Falconer
Pontlliw Primary School, 2003

128

Appendix

Penllergare or Penllergaer?

These place-name forms have given rise to much disputatious argument. Secondary sources vary as to the correct ascription with some contesting that the proper form should contain the suffix *gaer* and that *gare* is incorrect, being a distortion or corruption. Others contend that *Penllergare* is how the families associated with the mansion and the estate invariably spelled the name (the Prices, Llewelyns, Dillwyns and Dillwyn Llewelyns) and that this should be taken as the proper and authentic form. Several go further and dichotomise the two variants arguing that *gare* should apply to the mansion, demesne and the overall estate whereas *gaer* relates to the village of that name which emerged in the late nineteenth century. This distinction between estate and village is useful and should be seen as a pragmatic response to a debate which shows no signs of abating, particularly in the light of contemporary attempts on the part of the Penllergare Trust and others to recreate the historic core of the estate and rescue it from further decline and ultimate oblivion.

The earliest reference to the place-name contained in the Schedule B of the Penlle'rgaer Collection of Deeds & Documents, covering Glamorgan and Carmarthenshire, held at the National Library of Wales is *Penllegeer* (1608) when Griffith ap Evan is named as owner. By far the most common spelling that appears is *Penllergare*. Other variants are: *Penlergare; Penllargare; Penllegare; Penlle Gare; Penlleir Gare; Penllengare; Penllergaer, Penlle yr gare; Pen-lle-yr-Gare; Penlloyngare; Penllyrgare; Penllyr-Gare; Penllyrhare; Penlyrgare; Pennlergare; Pentle Gare; Tyr penlle yr gare and Tyr-penlle-yr gare*. (In addition, *Penller gar* appears in the 1650 survey of the lordship of Gower). In virtually every case the suffix *gare* is specified thus giving authenticity to the claim that historically and traditionally *Penllergare* is accurate when describing the estate.

The emergence of the village and modern-day community of Penllergaer date from the late nineteenth century from what historically had been 'Cors Eynon'. Indeed, the second edition of the six-inch Ordnance Survey map of 1900 names the area, somewhat schizophrenically, as 'Penll'ergaer or Gorseinon', which is reflective of the nascent urban changes transforming the district at that time. The place-name Gorseinon soon came to be applied to the greater urban area two miles west and south-west of the historic 'Cors Eynon' common. This left the way clear for the emerging community near 'Mynydd Gors Inon' or the common to be known as Penllergaer from about 1888-90 in contradistinction to the great estate on its doorstep, namely Penllergare. The latter spelling continues to be used by the family (based in Llysdinam Hall, Newbridge-on-Wye) as well as the agents to the estate to the present day. Much of the historic core of the estate however has in recent years been sold for modern property development. Parc Penllergaer is the clearest expression of this in the locality but as this is situated on what had formerly been Penllergare Home Farm land the appellation, if not inaccurate, merely compounds the toponomical confusion that can arise.

Jeff Childs, MA
An extract from a paper first published in
Morgannwg (Volume XLVII, 2003) The Journal of Glamorgan History

Index

[An index of contributors, significant names and places]

Note: page numbers in italics refer to illustrations

The Dillwyn Llewelyn Succession

Lewis Weston Dillwyn m. Mary Adams
1778-1855   1788-1865

Fanny
1808-1894
m. Matthew Moggridge

John Dillwyn Llewelyn
1810-1882
m. Emma Thomasina Talbot

William
1812-1819

Lewis Llewelyn
1814-1892
m. Bessie de la Beche

Mary
1816-1906
m. Revd. M. E. Welby

Sarah
1818-1828

Thereza
1834-1926

(Sir) John Talbot Dillwyn Llewelyn
1836-1927
m. Caroline Julia Hicks Beach

Emma Charlotte
1837-1928

William
1838-1866

Sybella
b.d. 1842

Elinor Amy
1844-1887

Lucy Caroline
1846-1920

Mary Caroline
1864-1873

John Michael
1866-1878

Gwendoline
1867-1944

William
1868-1893

(Sir) Charles Leyshon Dillwyn Llewelyn
1870-1951
m. Katherine Lister Venables

Henry
b.d. 1872

Gladys
1880-1959

John Lister
1897-1917

(Sir) Charles Michael Dillwyn Venables Llewelyn
1900-1976
m. Lady Delia Hicks Beach

George William
1910-1940

Agnes Barbara
1894-1998

Mary Julia

(Sir) John Michael Dillwyn Venables Llewelyn